Essays that Worked

Other books in this series:

Essays that Worked—For Business Schools
Essays that Worked—For Law Schools

Essays
THAT WORKED

50 Essays from Successful Applications
to the Nation's Top Colleges

Edited by
Boykin Curry and Brian Kasbar

Fawcett Columbine • New York

A Fawcett Columbine Book
Published by Ballantine Books
Copyright © 1986, 1990 by Boykin Curry and Brian Kasbar

All rights reserved under International and Pan-American Copyright Conventions. Published in the United States by Ballantine Books, a division of Random House, Inc., New York, and simultaneously in Canada by Random House of Canada Limited, Toronto. Originally published in somewhat different form by Mustang Publishing Co., Inc., in 1986.

Each essay in this book is used by permission of its author.

Library of Congress Catalog Card Number: 89-92591

ISBN: 0-449-90517-9

Cover design by Bill Geller

Manufactured in the United States of America
First Ballantine Books Edition: September 1990
10

For God, for Country, and for Yale.

And also, of course, for our parents.

Acknowledgments

A lot of people whose names aren't on the cover of this book spent many days (and some nights) to get it in your hands.

Fifty students allowed us to expose their most personal thoughts to thousands of readers who may not share their sympathies, backgrounds, or perspectives.

Admissions officers offered us essays and insights. Since this effort began four years and seven printings ago, officers at nineteen top schools have helped us: Yale, Harvard, Duke, Georgetown, Davidson, Williams, University of Pennsylvania, Rice, Grinnell, Stanford, Princeton, Oberlin, Berkeley, Wellesley, Johns Hopkins, Chapel Hill, Swarthmore, and Skidmore. William Hiss, Dean of Admissions at Bates College, even took the time to write a critique of our earlier book, and it appears in the preface to this edition.

Beth Siudut and Caroline Curry worked with the colleges to get new essays for the Ballantine edition. They polled the admissions officers for their reaction to the first edition, and they received important new advice.

Rollin Riggs at Mustang Publishing and Betsy Lerner at Ballantine helped revise the manuscript right up to the very, very latest deadline. Their patience and their nerves were tried and proved.

Contents

Preface to the Revised Edition

We first created *Essays That Worked* in 1986, when we came to learn how intimidated most high school students were by the college application process. Sure, the SATs and the interviews were tough, but what was really killing people were the application essays, which had grown dramatically in importance.

Designed to give admissions officers a look "behind the numbers" at the "real" applicant, the essay also gives students a terrific opportunity to wow the people who are deciding their college fate. As college admissions became increasingly competitive, the essay often became the deciding factor. Good essays were putting borderline students into the "Admit" pile. Bad essays were ruining even the best applications.

Applicants were so anxious because no one really knew what the admissions committees wanted when they asked for "a brief essay to tell us more about yourself." Many students thought they had to write for a bunch of fifty-year-old bald guys smoking pipes, and they wrote the most stiff, artificial prose imaginable.

We talked with admissions officers and discovered that all they wanted were honest, creative, expressive statements. They wanted an essay that gave special insight into an applicant's personality—insights they couldn't glean from grades and SAT scores. They showed us their favorite essays—essays that had "worked"—and the writing was anything but stiff and artificial. We thought if applicants could see what other successful candidates were writing about—inchworms, babysitting, Oreo cookies—they could break out of the "application mode" and express themselves more effectively on their college applications. We still believe that.

Unfortunately, our book did something else, too: It scared some applicants. "Those essays are so good," one told us, "that I don't think I'm up to it." And we didn't just hear from students. Admissions officers were concerned, too. The dean of admissions at Bates College wrote:

I confess when I looked through your earlier book, I had some misgivings. I find when I give workshops on the writing of college essays (and I probably do ten or twenty a year), young people are easily intimidated by brilliantly written, flashy or very perceptive writing. Often, far from giving them models and encouraging them, it seems to freeze them up and stall them out. They subconsciously throw up their hands and say, "I can't write like that," and more perniciously and subconsciously, "I guess I shouldn't go to demanding colleges." Incidentally, I find exactly the same reaction among faculty members and counselors if I offer them a series of beautifully written, erudite, balanced, witty and pithy recommendations. The effect is often the opposite of what I hope. So I would offer as a caveat for your new book the thought that we are not necessarily looking for the next Faulkner, the next Tolstoy. We are looking for students who write coherent, thoughtful, carefully organized, mechanically sound and hopefully imaginative prose. Sometimes that's flashy and creative, and sometimes it is not. I hasten to say that I don't mean this as a complaint or an attack on your previous book. It was well organized and had lots of wonderful writing samples in it. But we try to find some way to say to young people, "Write in your own voice." The central metaphor of admissions for me is not the Wizard of Oz, but theatrical lighting. That is to say, we hope students will not think they are to hide themselves behind a curtain and bellow into a microphone and saw at some ropes to create an image of themselves as powerful and unique. Rather we hope to have students think of themselves in the admissions process as being out on center stage front, with all of the different parts of the folder representing a different theatrical light to light up some particular facet of their personality or skills.

So let's get one thing straight: The essays in this book are not standards that you have to meet or beat in order to get into college. They simply represent the best fifty essays that we and admissions officers could gather out of hundreds of thousands of applications. (Indeed, our acceptance rate is much lower than Harvard's. We chose fifty essays from over one hundred thousand applications, while Harvard admits two thousand students from about ten thousand applicants. So you've got a much better chance of getting into Harvard than getting your essay into this book!)

Rather than try to "compete" against these essays, we hope you'll just use them for two things:

First, read all fifty essays and let them give you a sense of the wide range of what "works." Some essays are fifty words, some are five thousand. Some essays have dialogue, some are poems, and one is even a cartoon. You'll feel much less anxious about the process when you see how many options you have.

Second, let the essays inspire your creativity. Perhaps they will spark a memory or a creative connection. Remember, the best writers *read* great writing.

Getting into college is not a writing contest, and we certainly hope you won't write something only because you think it's the kind of essay that would get into this book. Worse yet, we hope you won't forgo writing an essay because you know it *wouldn't* get into this book. Your goal is simply to communicate something new and meaningful about yourself to someone who knows almost nothing. It's a great opportunity, so don't waste it.

And *relax*.

Boykin Curry
Brian Kasbar

Essays that Worked

Introduction

You are an admissions officer at Harvard, Duke, or Stanford, and it is two o'clock in the morning of April 9. Your desk is somewhere beneath a huge stack of papers. Your eyes are tired and red. Mechanically you open the next application folder, and again you force yourself to read:

I am constantly striving to expose myself to every opportunity to become a person with a deep understanding of my own values and of the environment in which I find myself. I have participated in a broad range of activities, and I have endeavored to become ever more versatile and tolerant while at the same time solidifying my own ideals. . . .

You cannot go on. But you must, because the deadline for notifying applicants is just a few days away. The prospect: another long night reading vague, boring, pompous essays. You slowly bow your head and rest it in your hands, wishing for a different job.

Suddenly a gust of wind blows through an open window, upsetting the pile of applications. As four hundred essays flutter around the room, you notice a page with the recipe for cranberry bread.

A recipe? Cranberry bread?

Curious, you pick up the essay and start to read, and you smile:

4 c. flour
2 c. sugar
3 t. baking powder
1 pkg. cranberries

. . . Not only is the following an overview of my personality but also a delicious recipe.

First the flour and sugar need to be sifted together into a large bowl. Flour reminds me of the powder snow that falls in the West. I was born and raised in Pennsylvania where our snow falls more like sugar, granular and icy, and makes us hardy skiers unlike those spoiled by Western snow. Cold weather is also conducive to reading . . .

Finally, a student you would want to *meet*, someone who dares to express herself creatively, rather than simply recite the same old litany of high school achievements and adolescent philosophies. Finally, an interesting essay!

As you finish the "recipe" and read through the rest of her application, you start to feel much better. Decent grades, good test scores, solid recommendations—you've seen better, but it's certainly respectable. And then there's this fantastic essay, evidence of an inventive and independent mind. The essay makes your decision easy. You put her folder into a box marked "Admit," and you look forward to discussing her with the Admissions Committee tomorrow.

This is an exaggeration, of course, but it makes an important point. Admissions officers are very human. They will laugh at a funny joke, and they will get excited over a well-written account of a close game. They may even shed a tear if you pull them through a tragedy. On the other hand, admissions officers will become bored and irritated as quickly as anyone by essays that are dull and blatantly self-serving.

When we first started working on this book, we collected hundreds of essays. Filled with enthusiasm on our first night, we started reading. Several hours later, after ten class elections, eight trips to Europe, and five solutions to the problem of world hunger, we were praying for an essay that was *fun* to read, an essay that might make us laugh or think or understand. But please, God, not another piece on "what-I-learned-by-working-so-hard-as-yearbook-editor."

We quickly understood why the smallest bit of wit or creativity can strike an admissions officer as exceptional brilliance.

In its own way, each essay in this book is enlightening and entertaining. It informs the reader without boring him. Since these essays are among the best in America, you shouldn't be intimidated if your writing doesn't seem nearly so brilliant. (Our essays didn't make the book, either.) Some of these pieces are beautifully written, some are a bit awkward, but each gives a tiny flash into the lives of fifty ordinary students much like yourself. Each essay tells you something about its author that you wouldn't learn from reading grade transcripts and lists of extracurricular activities.

To be sure, many of the essays are "self-serving." They describe high school achievements and try to reinforce the rest of the application. But each piece also brings a special focus to the personality and mind of the writer, and that's exactly what admissions officers want to see.

Every college application that we have seen has plenty of space for you to list your grades and all your accomplishments. But the essay is the only section where you have total control. Your grades, your scores, your activities—they're history, and there is nothing you can do about them when you sit down to fill in the blanks. The essay, however, offers a precious opportunity for you to express your individuality, so don't squander the chance by just repeating what the rest of the application already shows. The essay is your chance to say, "Hey, *this* is me! I'm creative/witty/insecure/perceptive/enthusiastic/shy/adventurous—and all of the above."

The admissions officer wants to know the real you, and what makes you tick. What do you see differently from your friends? Why do you want to go to college? Do you talk to yourself? Hate sunny days? Take baths instead of showers? Still forget when to use "whom"? You don't have to vacation in the Orient or ski in the Olympics to have an amusing or interesting perspective. Some of the best essays are about seemingly trivial things, like inchworms, missing socks, and Elvis. By finding the profound in the mundane, a writer can tell the admissions officer more about his personality than all the teacher references ever could.

So consider what you do each day, what you want, what you notice. The perfect essay may not pop into your head immediately, and you may have to write quite a few drafts before it clicks. But writing a good essay can make you think about the Meaning of Life, or about the junk accumulating under your bed. It can be illuminating, it can be fun, and it might even get you in.

An Interview
with an Admissions Officer

He still had a hundred essays to read before 6:00 p.m., and he was beginning to grow tired. My interview with him would offer a brief break from the Herculean task of narrowing ten thousand applicants to a freshman class of nine hundred.

"I hope your book works," he joked, "so maybe next year I won't have to read five hundred essays about the yearlong drama of being student council president. I'm sorry, but successful car washes just don't make for enthralling reading."

I smiled. He rubbed his eyes.

"On a Wednesday in the middle of March this job gets tough. Sometimes it seems that there are only four types of essays: the 'class president' essay, the 'I lost but learned' sports essay, the 'I went to Europe and learned how complex the world is' essay, and the good old 'being yearbook editor sure is hard work' essay. When I read one of those, it takes amazing willpower to get to the third paragraph."

"So sometimes you don't read the whole essay?" I asked.

"No comment," he replied, changing the subject. "I wish students would realize that when they write they should have something to say. They should try to present their values and priorities by writing on a subject that really means something to them, because, other than the essay, all I have is a bunch of test scores and activities: ten thousand sets of numbers and facts. I'd like to be able to see beyond that. I want to see what makes someone tick."

"But couldn't that be dangerous?" I asked. "What if someone writes something really bizarre, just to avoid being 'boring'? Can strange ideas or comments hurt an applicant?"

6

"Well, if someone expressed homicidal tendencies, it would probably have a negative effect. Still, you'd be surprised how tolerant we are. A few years ago, we had a kid from Palestine apply. In his essay, he endorsed Yassir Arafat and the PLO. As far as he was concerned, Israel had usurped the rightful land of his people and should be treated as a criminal state. The admissions officer who covered the Middle East was an Orthodox Jew. Not only did the student get in, but he graduated with honors in political science.

"In fact, being offbeat or daring is usually a plus, as long as the student stays in control of his writing. The essays which are most effective seize a topic with confidence and imagination. Too many applicants treat their essay like a minefield. They walk around on tiptoes, avoiding anything controversial. Of course, the essay comes out two-dimensional, flat, and boring. It seems like many essays have been read, proofread, and reproofread until all the life has been sucked out. I wish kids would just relax and not try to guess what the admissions committee is looking for. As soon as they start playing that game, they're going to lose. The essay won't be from the heart, and it won't work.

"The great essays—good writers discussing something of personal importance—stick out like diamonds in a coal bin. When we're sorting through the last few hundred applications, an essay that sticks out in an admissions officer's mind has got to help the applicant who wrote it."

"How important is it to be a good writer?" I asked.

"Writing style tells you a lot about the way a person thinks. I like when a student brings a sense of style to a piece, as a good essayist or editorial writer would do. I've always advocated reading the essays of E. B. White as a means of preparing for writing the essay. I also suggest that students read the editorial pages of the local newspaper. But we never discount the student who writes a simple, even awkward, essay which is sincere and moving.

"That's why I urge students to write as they would in a diary or a letter to a friend. When you write a letter, you may ramble, but when you're finished, your letter sounds like something you would really say."

"So an honest, personal essay is best?"

"No, there is no 'best' type of essay. But when a 'personal' essay is done well, it can be very effective. The best I've ever read was written about fifteen years ago by a football recruit. His application was perfect: high school all-America quarterback, president of his class, 3.8 GPA, and a mile-long list of extracurriculars. But his essay was about his stuttering. He wrote about his loneliness in junior high, about the girls who laughed at him, and about the wall he built around himself. Since football was something he really loved, he buried himself in it, spending afternoons in the weight room and nights in front of a mirror, practicing words and signals so he wouldn't embarrass himself by stuttering on the field.

"When you put an essay like that beside one of those self-absorbed recitals of high school achievements—there's just no comparison."

I decided to change the subject a little. "What really irritates you in an essay?"

"Arrogance and pretentiousness are bad, but the only thing that really bugs me is when a student doesn't put his personality into an essay. I always hear parents and students complain that colleges don't look so much at the individual student as they do at scores, grades, and class rank, so I'm disappointed when students don't take advantage of the only place in the application that allows them to express their individuality."

"Okay, then," I asked, "what do you really like to see?"

"I always enjoy essays where the author realizes that he's writing for an audience of real human beings. I also like essays with a touch of excitement and enthusiasm, and I like an applicant who demonstrates the ability to look at himself from the outside. And, of course, wit never hurts."

"So should applicants try to write funny essays?"

" 'Funny' isn't a good word, because there's a fine line between something that is humorous and something that is obnoxious or inappropriate. I much prefer an essay that is amusing because of its insight over one in which a kid is trying to write a string of one-liners—that rarely works."

I paused for a moment, thinking how to word my next question tactfully. "How much of a 'sell' do you expect?"

"How much do I expect? Tons. I expect that most kids will try to wow me with their accomplishments, even though I could just look at their activities list if I really want to know. Each year we have enough valedictorians, class presidents, and team captains to fill our freshman class five times. With that many talented kids, it's hard to impress me by listing your glorious achievements.

"How much of a 'sell' would I like? None. We enroll people, not cars, and I want more than a list of 'added features.' I am less interested in hearing what a student has done than hearing *why* he does what he does. Anything that comes across as a 'sell' is negative. If what comes through is a healthy self-confidence in your own accomplishments, then that's positive.

"Also, of course, a hard 'sell' can really backfire if the essay is not consistent with the rest of the application. A student once wrote an angry essay about social injustice and how the world should feed and clothe the poor. So I checked her list of activities. She had never been involved in any charities or community service programs, so I was pretty skeptical of her true feelings. No one likes hypocrisy, so if an applicant's record doesn't back up the essay, it can add a large negative factor into my decision.

"A common theme which is both uninteresting and unrevealing is participation in organizations which are 'in' at the time, such as SADD and SafeRides. Also, stating that you were listed in *Who's Who of American High School Seniors* only tells me that you were willing to pay."

I decided to go for all the marbles. "All said, what is the best essay?"

"What works the best? Honesty, brevity, risk taking, self-revelation, imaginativeness, and fine writing: many of the attributes which are edited out when you ask someone's opinion of your college essay. If a student reads his application before mailing it and can say 'this sounds like me,' then he's probably written the best essay possible. Students should feel more comfortable trusting their instincts. Nine times out of ten, an essay that feels good to the writer will be good for the reader, too. And that should make the process better for all those involved—as essay writers or essay readers!"

(The quotes from the "admissions officer" above were compiled from the comments of all the admissions officers we interviewed.)

The Essays

For organizational purposes only, we divided the essays into ten groups: essays about relationships, travel, and various obstacles; offbeat essays and self-description essays; essays about home, realizations, intellectual thought, activities, and the college application process. Please bear in mind that this grouping is *totally artificial*. You don't have to write an essay that would fit neatly into one of these categories.

We created the introductions to each group of essays from the comments submitted by admissions officers about the essays they sent. As well as being a fine piece of writing on its own, an essay might also exemplify a "type." For instance, the piece about an inchworm by Jamie Mayer (page 117) is a great example of the "thought essay," which is a fairly popular topic. So if you are planning to write this type of essay, pay special attention to the comments in the group's introduction, as well as to the styling of the essay.

Of course, the essay question may limit your range of responses. Most colleges ask for something vague and open-ended, such as "Please write something that will tell us more about you." For that, you could write about practically anything. Other schools have more specific questions, like "Which adjective would describe you by those who know you best?" or even "If you could have dinner with one famous person, who would it be and why?" Though answers to topics like these must be tightly structured, they still give you the chance to develop a unique and memorable image.

The essays are reproduced exactly as they were submitted, though, of course, the typeface and spacing are different. (Also, a couple were handwritten.) We did not correct punctuation, spelling, or grammar errors in the essays. But note that very rarely would such correction be needed.

Finally, a warning. We know that no one would be foolish enough to copy any of these essays verbatim. However, some readers might be tempted to take an essay and "change it around a little" to suit his application. We hope you know how stupid that would be. For one thing, stealing an idea or a phrase from an essay in this book would be dishonest. For another thing, it would seriously jeopardize your chance of getting into college. Remember, this is a very popular book. Most admissions officers have read it and are familiar with each essay. No admissions officer would ever admit a plagiarist.

The following pages demonstrate the creative potential of the college application essay. We hope they will give you the confidence to write a bold, personal piece that will help an admissions officer see why you're special. Enjoy the essays, study them, and let them be a catalyst for your own creativity.

Before You Start to Write

1. Begin thinking of essay topics early in the fall.

2. Write a time line of your life, noting special dates and important events.

3. Make a list of five or six possible essay topics and discuss them with your friends, parents, teachers, etc.

4. Find a quiet place, and "write" the essay in your mind.

5. Everyone procrastinates to some extent. Be sure to give yourself plenty of time to work on the essay before the deadline.

Essays About Relationships

It's said that we are the sum of our relationships. Having read your scores, grades, and recommendations, there are few questions more important to a college than "How does this person get along with the people around her?" and "Does this person *recognize* how she lives with the people around her?"

If you're going to write an essay about relationships, there's no need to pat yourself on the back with platitudes about how open-minded and compassionate you are. In fact, writing about your selfishness may reveal more sensitivity than writing about the time you helped a little old lady across the street.

In the first essay—one of the most powerful we've seen—the writer speaks to all of us about the paradox of jealousy. Describing one brief moment, she expresses herself better than three pages of long-winded analysis ever could.

The next applicant struggles between principles and emotions of family and ideology. It doesn't matter whether you (or the admissions officer) *agree* with her conclusions. She brings us through her personal battle and vividly shows us what is important to her.

Marie Louise Buhler has created a character with a fullness usually found only in a short story. She has cared enough about someone to really *think* about him, a rare enough characteristic. In addition, her writing style is excellent. A writing expert at Yale said, "The last sentence deserves reading and rereading—for its stunning control of rhythm, and its wonderful ending on one lonely word (grammatically isolated, on the far side of the comma), 'alone.' "

People who never read the Bible still know the parables, because they make moral lessons real with stories we can get hold of. The writers in this group of essays don't just say, "I know a lot about jealousy," "I have strong principles," "My mother is a strong woman," or "I am sensitive enough to really understand someone." They bring us along on their paths of discovery and make their personalities come alive.

Name Withheld

Her hand reached for the paper as it lay rustling in the breeze from the open window, and I resisted the urge I felt to snatch it from her fingers. Her eyebrows rose and I could feel her eyes laughing as she held her lips still and pressed together. The words were blurring on the sheet, and I drew my knees up against my eyes, shutting her away, searching for a way out. How could a sister be so cruel? I wondered. Her full blond hair brushed heavily against her cheek.

She scanned the thin white paper for eternity-seconds ticked away by the rhythmic brush of the pine on the screen, then turned her green eyes to rest on mine. She pitied me. I could not write, I was not creative, I did not win her poetry awards. She placed a bone-slim hand on my knee as I screamed at her for invading me, screamed in the pain of always having her better me, condescend to me. The silence echoed. I retreated to the plastic comfort of knowing I would never be the insensitive person she was.

She sat down facing me, searching to see what I was thinking. Her smile was kind and thoughtful, and I knew she was going to say something unbearably reassuring. I opened my eyes, they melted blue, and I stared at her and I loved her and I sang and cried in words she couldn't hear, would never hear. I pushed back my hair and I stood up and I left her there, sitting on a window seat, in front of a wind-swept pine.

Name Withheld

When people hear what's left of my accent and ask, "Are you British?" I'm never quite sure what to say. My mother is Scottish and my father is Jewish-American; I'm the product of whatever synthesis can possibly come of two disparate cultures. My parents are a classic example of opposites attracting, and they get along just fine. But contrasts that complement each other in a marriage don't always work so well together when they're in the same person. I've often felt the opposing characteristics and traditions of each of their backgrounds in conflict inside me.

Growing up in Berkeley has reinforced in me my father's tradition of social activism, and muted the socially conservative Presbyterianism of my mother's upbringing. After all, Berkeley has Malcolm X Middle School, Stephen Biko Plaza, Ho Chi Minh Park, and an annual Gay-Lesbian Day parade. Both of our two local political camps are to the left of the National Democratic Party, and we have more ethnic restaurants than we do Republicans. Street artists sell their hand carved incense holders, silver peace-symbol pendants, and T-shirts tie-dyed in psychedelic colors up and down Telegraph Avenue. Berkeley tolerates anything—except intolerance. So I found myself quite unprepared when I encountered precisely that in my own family on a visit to Scotland last summer.

I hadn't seen my Scottish relatives in five years. The sight of the grey North Sea and the stone dikes running low over tilled fields in Aberdeenshire released a flood of memories. I remembered visiting as a little girl: sitting in the strawberry field gorging myself, helping to drive sheep into a market-bound trailer, leaping off the barn rafters into a mountain of grain. Uncle Rob, my mother's younger brother, would amaze me by apparently grabbing only my ears and lifting me high into the air. Then he'd laugh and tousle my curly hair, so much like his own. So I looked forward to seeing him again.

When I did, it was in the morning-room of his comfortable

country home inn. In the course of conversation over coffee, Uncle Rob announced, "The way things are going, pretty soon there won't be any real women left to stay home where they belong and raise children." I thought he might be joking at first; "Come on Uncle Rob . . ." I laughed. But my mother caught my eye with a warning glance, and I knew he was serious. He didn't stop there. By the time his coffee cup was empty he had weighed in strongly against homosexuals, blacks, and liberal thought in general. It took every ounce of self control I had to heed my mother's cue.

I was angry and confused as we all went through to lunch. My mother sensed my distress and whispered, "You can cope dear. You'll have to. Remember, he is your uncle." But as we sat down I wondered that I didn't explode. I wanted to erase the last ten minutes of conversation so he could still be my Uncle Rob and lift me up by my ears, which were now burning with frustration and indignation. I wished he'd never said any of it; now that he had, I thought, things could never be the same again. I knew there was nothing I could do to change his mind. My favorite uncle was a bigot, plain and simple. How could I love someone and hate everything he believed? How could I claim to have beliefs, if I allowed exceptions to them?

I was still struggling with these questions when we went out to the farm one more time before flying back home. Uncle Rob showed me the grain dryer and the milking barn, and I helped him innoculate a herd of cows. We didn't talk politics. When it came time to say goodbye, I gave him a hug and a kiss and he laughed like I remembered.

On the plane back to Berkeley, I realized that I had grown up in an area which was, in its own way, as insular and sheltered as Aberdeenshire. I had known, of course, that there were intolerant people in the world. But somehow, in my mind they had all worn KKK hoods. It was easy to hate and disdain them from afar; I thought of them as stupid and cruel, nothing like my uncle. Coming face to face with someone I loved and respected, but who believed the unspeakable, made me realize how narrow-minded this view is. Passing harsh judgment on people based on a litmus test of their politics risked making my world smaller just as Uncle Rob's racism makes his.

I do love my Uncle Rob. I'm sorry that he won't know the richness of living among different cultures, and that he'll probably miss out on meeting some interesting blacks, Jews, and homosexuals. I still think his nativism and bigotry are a danger and a shame. But while the nature of friendship is that it begins and ends by choice, I didn't choose to be related to my uncle, and I can't choose not to be. It's permanent; the only choice I have is whether to make the best of it. To enjoy the certainty of love and commitment that family life brings, I have to accept the members of my family as they are. I decided that if Uncle Rob were prepared to put up with a niece who must seem pretty radical to a Scottish farmer, I could put up with him.

I feel like a puzzle, made up of pieces I'm discovering on the road to adulthood. One of the pieces I've found is a commitment to social justice; another is a need to feel close to my Scottish relatives, despite their traditional respect for the status quo. Ironically, it was in that same Scottish tradition of acceptance that I found a way to fit the two pieces together.

Marie Louise Buhler

He is the strangest person I have ever met, not simply
eccentric, truly strange. He stumbled into my life (or rather I
into his) the day Oma took me into that laundromat. With the
wind at my back, I flew through the doors into a room of sticky,
moist air that vibrated with the hum of a dozen different cycles.
He was perched on the nearest dryer: checked shirt hanging
open, light-blue polyester pants too high above the sockless feet
encased in the inevitable sneakers. He guessed from my
"outlandish" clothes that I was American (what other five year
old in a small North German town would wear Raggedy-Ann
skirts?) He asked on a hunch if I wasn't the little girl whose
father was a lawyer in the Navy and whose mother was a friend
of Uncle Gert, his own good friend. I was. Being a precocious
child who told every embarrassing family secret to any stranger
who cared to listen, I struck up a fine conversation with him. He
complimented me on my German and then Oma towed me back
out into the rain.

I never gave that incident another thought until Uncle Henry
moved to the States and became an integral part of my Sunday
afternoons and my family. I hear him laughing downstairs. I see
his shoddy pants and frayed shirts, his silver hair as a Prussian
soldier's (my mother says) and his round, red face with its little
mustache. It's the face of an English squire. That's what he
should be, a country lord with a fixed income and nothing to do
but read and take long walks instead of eking out a living
keeping books for Palmer Ford. I guess I really don't know much
about him. Nobody does and that's the way he likes it. What I
do know convinces me that if ever a man were born in the
wrong century, it's Uncle Henry. He is a chivalrous knight.
Once he was engaged and in love, but when he heard another
richer man wanted to marry the girl he gave her up, *told* her to
marry the guy and moved. Some people call that stupid,
throwing away happiness with both hands, and maybe it was,
but it was *noble*. He says a man's life is over at thirty-five

unless he's married. Accordingly, he lives like a monk, always referring to himself as "this old man" and remarking that he can feel the "cool wind of the grave" blowing towards him. His pleasures are mainly scholarly. He lives in his Shakespeare and his French studies. He also lives in his coke and bourbon. Not, I guess to "wash the dust of the road" from his throat, as he puts it, but to wash away too vivid memories of war and loss. And it works, and remembering the good times and his beloved homeland, he bursts into old German songs which he bellows at the top of his lungs no matter where he is. When my sister and I were little, he embarrassed us and we pleaded with Uncle Henry to be "normal". He hasn't stopped laughing about that one since. Our begging had no effect and I'm glad now; I love his idiosyncracies. He is a Catholic who regularly speaks aloud with God, whom he asks to forgive "this old man" for never attending services. Evolution offends him, he won't even consider that we are related to animals. Uncle Henry believes that he is, and he is, a race apart. On the subject of modern medicine he is a skeptic, and though he should see someone about his blood pressure, he has staunchly refused to do so for the past twenty years. I love this man who sends me out of the room when he is going to tell a dirty joke, who advises my mother to give the two of us cold showers to keep us out of trouble, who calls me his "pale beauty" and tells me to eat more. Everybody likes him, but no one understands him. He lets nobody in. And in the end all he has left are his books and his bourbon and his memories, as he sits in a crummy shack of an apartment with gaping holes in the roof, alone.

Robin Bernstein

January 1987

My mother is a feisty woman who argues with cashiers and plumbers and generally gets her way. My brother and I don't like to go with her to fast food restaurants because she invariably fights with the teenager at the cash register and ends up calling the manager. Although this drives my family crazy, I think we respect her for standing up for herself and not letting anyone push her around.

There was exactly one time I was afraid she might lose a fight. This October, across an oval dinner table, my mother told us she had breast cancer. I remember looking down at the chicken leg on my plate and realizing it would go uneaten.

We wobbled to the living room. My mother arranged my brother, father, and me on the couch and put herself on the piano stool so she could see us all at once. I felt posed, like for a portrait. And my mother was not going to be in that portrait. We cried for three hours.

Then my brother retreated into the television and my mother and father went to their room. I didn't know what to do. I don't mean that I didn't know what to do to make things better or what to do to survive the next few weeks that would encompass her mastectomy. I mean I didn't know what to do with the rest of the evening. Ordinary activities seemed grossly inappropriate, and unusual activities required more than I had to give. I was cried out, talked out, and wrung out. All I felt was a giant vacuum where my guts had been. I couldn't remember what I'd been like the day before.

I spent the rest of the evening rereading my sixth grade diary. It was funny to recognize myself on the pages. While the spelling and handwriting had changed over the years, the flow, sentence structure, idea associations, and feelings were all unmistakably me. I read until I fell asleep.

When she awoke in the recovery room, my mother heard a nurse complaining she was getting the flu. She asked the nurse to put on a mask before approaching. The nurse became nasty, and my mother took her name. When they wheeled her to us, she was furious. She explained the whole fight in nearly the same way she had recounted horror stories involving plumbers or auctioneers. That's when I knew she was going to be all right. And she is.

Andrew C. Hiss

My family gives advice, discussion, argument and thought, but never orders. I was never pushed to become an olympic athlete, a great artist or genius. My family felt that it was not their role to decide who I was to become; with only their input I was left to decipher the world with my own eyes, make my own judgments and decide for myself what I would become.

My grandfather and I had more in common than I have ever had with anyone else, and my interests have grown from him: art, philosophy, religion and culture—people and the way they act in society. My grandfather had emphysema; he was emaciated, constantly wheezed and trailed behind him through the house yards and yards of clear plastic oxygen tubing. When he began to deteriorate, I consciously spent time with him. Every day after school, I would walk through the dirty, slushy snow of Auburn to his house, let myself in and call, "Hey, gramp." He would look up from his book, unwrap his leg which was usually entwined in oxygen tubing and ask me how my day was. From there the two of us, like two old fishermen around a fire, would get lost in discussion. We would talk and argue about history, politics, current events and art. Something said would remind him of an event long ago which would start a chain reaction of never-ending hilarious stories. His stories would get me laughing so hard with warmth and often embarrassment that I would turn an exaggerated shade of scarlet, and the two of us would have to take ten minute breathing breaks. Most of my interests, my artistic ability, my sense of humor, and much of what I like most about life are all linked to him. Although my grandfather's influence has helped shape many of my interests and ideas, I lack his greatest gift of all: his company.

My family has also influenced my views about racism, but once again they never preached. My parents very sneakily influenced my feelings towards racism by adopting my sister Kate. By growing up with a black sister, I lost all conception of race. I do not see blacks, whites, reds or yellows; I just see people.

However, because I had no conception of racism I did not really understand how it existed. I had seen racism in "Roots" and a few of the books I had read, but I had never come in contact with it and therefore, did not acknowledge its existence. But recently I met a young boy who was very proud and excited to show me his "nigger beater." The device turned out to be a solid piece of oak, about two and one half feet long with iron ribbon carefully laced around the top. When I asked him what he was going to do with such a menacing weapon, he replied with a "tough guy" face, "Whale on people who come after me." I thought, with a name like "nigger beater", what kind of connotation does such a weapon give blacks in this country? As someone to be constantly beware of? As someone out to take advantage and to harm? This incident rattled me. This boy has certainly never spoken to and probably only seen blacks on T.V. (Kate is one of perhaps five black teenagers in Lewiston-Auburn). This boy seemed racist, not from experience but from ignorance and fear. Sometimes I think of Kate and of this boy with his "nigger beater."

I am never worried about living up to my family's expectations; their only expectation of me is to be myself. My family gave me an initial push and released me to drift down my own river, at a current of my choice, in a raft built by my hands, with a destination concocted of my dreams.

Essays About Travel

To hear some admissions officers tell it, they get at least one million essays about travel every year. Approximately eight hundred thousand are about a trip to Europe that taught the writer "how complex the world is" or "how all people have the same hopes and dreams." One hundred thousand are about an emotional trip to Jerusalem. The remaining hundred thousand are about journeys to Africa, Asia, or South America.

And every year, of those one million essays, maybe three are interesting. Face it—how many times do you think one admissions officer can stand to read about a two-week vacation in Paris?

It's not that your trips are inherently boring, and it's not that the lessons you can learn from travel are automatically trite. Rather, most essays about travel are dull because they lack the detail necessary to bring the reader on the trip *with* you. Just saying you went to France and saw a lot of old stuff is not exciting or insightful. But describing your relationship with your ninety-one-year old grandmother who lives in the countryside and doesn't speak English *is* exciting. Interesting and telling detail is the key to a good travel essay—indeed, to all good essays.

This is precisely why travel is such a difficult subject to choose for your application essay. The emotions we feel when we travel are so deep that it takes an exceptional writer to express them without falling into cliché. Not one of the writers in this section said, "I learned so-and-so on my trip to Dublin." Instead, each student brings the reader through a memorable experience and lets the reader actually "see" the scenes and feel the emotions himself.

John Sigalos, the first essayist, could have written, "When I lived in France, I met a dear old woman, and I learned that friendship and love are the same in every language." Fortunately, he didn't. Notice how much more effective his essay is when he describes one small incident instead of his whole trip. He tells us about the crucifix in his friend's room, about the wrinkles in her cheek as she kisses him good-bye. Detail, detail, detail! His imagery is so powerful that we can almost feel the tears sting his eyes as he leaves.

The second writer does another superb job with imagery. She doesn't just tell you about the frustration of a language barrier, she *shows* you by describing the time when she bumped into a stranger on a crowded street. She brings the Chinese people to life for us, and that's what makes her essay work.

In the third essay, the applicant shows us an America we may have never noticed. We think of Africa as a mysterious land full of adventure, but this writer is from Africa, and he treats Lancaster, Pennsylvania, as an "alien and magnificent" destination. He makes our point perfectly. How exciting would it be to say, "My annual trip to Pennsylvania gives me a new perspective on life"? But when he describes the "sixty foot yellow 'M' " on the roadside and "Super Large, Grape Flavoured Hubba Bubba Bubblegum," he shows us the America he sees brilliantly, and what he sees says a lot about him.

Catherine Sustana also makes a trip within America sound sensational and inspiring. She didn't go to France or Africa or China, but her anecdotes about travels in the West are superb. This is a great essay to read if you feel you've never been anywhere exciting. The truth is, *everywhere* is exciting, if you know how to appreciate it.

John L. Sigalos

She is four feet six inches tall. Her wrinkled body stands wrapped in a hand-knit sweater, a figure from some classic painting. On her feet are heavy, black leather shoes with thick soles, like the ones on my white-haired grandfather in the old yellowing photographs. She wears her stockings with unspoken pride, despite the numerous runs and tears that spot the blue-veined and sinewy legs.

I bend down to embrace her. I feel her hands on my shoulders. Beaten by ninety-one years of work, calloused and clawlike, they rest on my bent back as if enjoying a few moments rest. I embrace her the traditional three times, touching my smooth cheek against hers. It is grooved and worn yet feels cool and softly innocent against my warm skin.

Standing up, I look around the apartment. The one room has an ancient gas stove and oven, whose door moans when opened, a stained and cracking porcelain sink, a chess board-size table covered with a white, starchy linen, and in the corner stands the mahogany armoire, elegant and proud with its sculpted panels. Inside, I know, is the china set she received as a wedding present from her parents, seventy years ago. She showed me, one Saturday afternoon while we waited for the "Chaussons A Pommes"[1] to cook, these last souvenirs of youth and love, each paper thin plate and tiny tea cup with a cursive "L" in gold letters, for "LeFevre."

The bedroom is a space as large as a closet, with a mattress covered box in the corner and a barely-illuminating bronze lamp attached to the plaster wall. Above the waist-high oak dresser is the only decoration in the two room dwelling—a blackened iron crucifix, expressionless in it's heavy age, forged by her blacksmith father a century ago.

"Alors, c'est le depart,"[2] she says in a cracked voice saturated with the choppy Breton accent. Her warming eyes, two chips of carved and polished turquoise, flicker over my blushing face.

"Mais oui,"[3] I answer with confidence, trying to hide the

sudden tingle in the back of my throat. No, I won't cry. I imagine her embracing, with smooth and strong arms, her young farmer husband as he packed his suitcase and left for Verdun in 1916. Then embracing with a weakening grip her two tall, dark-skinned sons as they enlisted in the resistance in 1940. Now I, in my turn, stand before her. I feel like a single goodbye in a lifetime of goodbyes, a small wound on a body torn with red and vicious scars. No, I won't cry.

"Eh, ben, c'est la deuxieme fois que je vois partir de chez moi les Americains."[4] Until now she has been toying clumsily with the fraying hem of her black wool sweater. She looks up. Thick tears glaze her porcelain eyes. I am for an instant the handsome, un-shaven American soldier marching through Chateaubourg in 1945, who stopped to give the crying four-foot six-inch woman a white rose and an army-issue pack of Camels. Looking past my green Izod shirt, faded Levis, and ratty Nike sneakers, her water-color blue eyes see a great-grandson that she never had, the boy that spent Tuesday afternoons pushing a shopping cart through the local supermarket with her, the loud "taquineur"[5] that got a kick out of naively denying her true stories about the two World Wars that raged on her own front lawn.

"C'est la deuxieme fois",[6] she repeats. I can't stop my watering eyes from looking away. I search my French vocabulary for something to say. My mouth is dry, and I stutter abruptly, "Merci, merci pour tout."

1 = A desert pastry like apple pie
2 = "So, looks like it's time for you to leave."
3 = "Looks that way."
4 = "Well, this is the second time I've seen the Americans pull through Chateaubourg."
5 = Teaser, person who likes to tease
6 = "It's the second time."

Name Withheld

"Hello, my name is Lin Yan. How do you do? What is your name?"

She was wearing a bright red polyester dress, ankle stockings, and sandals with a slight heel. She had on rectangular, dark-rimmed glasses. Her long, shiny, black hair was neatly braided in the back and fastened with a plastic mouse that had eyes that jiggled as she moved her head. I felt genuinely welcomed when she smiled and reached out to shake my hand.

Lin Yan became my best friend at camp in China last summer. I got another letter from her yesterday. She is now studying very hard, reviewing all that she has learned in the past five years for her exam in July. She has very little time for T.V. or playing because of so much work. Answering one of my questions, she wrote that during the Cultural Revolution she rarely ate eggs or meat, her parents always worried about money at the end of the month, and her father "was said a bad person because he had said something true." She continued writing, "It was a really hard time, but I think it useful to have trained me a very strong girl. Now if I have any difficulties, I always have confidence to overcome them. I have a strong belief, if someone has done her best in doing something, she would be satisfied no matter if it success or failure. I'm trying my best now." She always seems to have a positive attitude and to be motivated by her faith in the future. While I was there, we talked about starting a joint technology firm in our two countries when we get older. We dreamed together.

Friendship like this enriches life. It changes common events into exciting and stimulating experiences. Fortunately, my family has always valued these experiences much more than material items. Until recently my father worked for a foundation in the South. We travel together rather than have two cars and a color T.V. or belong to a Country Club. I have never taken a luxury travel tour, but our family reads and explores the cities, villages, and countrysides on our own. No guidebook I have ever read mentions the Spanish waitress who taught me to whistle one of her songs; or the Palestini boys who accepted our challenge to a soccer game on a Left Bank plaza in Paris; or the lady at St. James Park who could feed pigeons by holding bread crust between her teeth and who taught us to be gentle with the birds; or the bald Frenchman at the gas station who was so patient after we mistakenly filled our car with "gazoil," instead of "essence," and we had to be towed to a garage.

My goal in life is to develop as many friendships as possible, to share, question, and learn as much as I can. When I returned from China this summer, people asked about the food, the shopping, our living conditions, and frequently the Great Wall. Many of our friends who had traveled there told us of a horrible time because of the dirty utensils, the lack of hot water, or the frustration of a difficult language barrier. They could not conceive of what we had endured with only a laugh! We were there to gain from the experience, to get in touch with the culture, and to make new friends—not to be entertained. I wanted to love and grow and get to know people, understand their way of life. I reached out and was met eagerly.

One day I was walking a bike through a crowd of people and accidentally knocked into a tiny man at my side. Immediately I said with my American pronunciation, "Dway-bu-chi! (excuse me)," and his solemn expression that might have been a cold, annoyed stare turned into an encouraging, delighted laugh as he clapped and pointed me out to his friends. He must have told them what had happened because they all then laughed, gave me the "thumbs up" signal, cheered, and repeated over and over, "Dway-bu-chi! Dway-bu-chi!" I wish my vocabulary were a lot larger, so I could have continued talking with the amiable men.

Another afternoon after a picnic lunch, three friends and I found a quiet plateau overlooking the green mountains where Mongolian farmers were grazing their cattle. One friend had brought his guitar, and we sat down singing softly. Soon a group of Mongolian children and adults shyly approached us, stayed for some time, smiled and left. When we were again alone, an old woman with the most pleasant toothless smile climbed up the steep slope from the village down below and joined us. She had a wind-beaten face, thin black hair tied under a scarf, and sturdy, hard-worked hands, one holding a bouquet of colorful wild flowers and the other a black iron cane. We motioned for her to sit, and she did. After many songs, her favorite being the *Sound of Music*, she shook our hands and motioned good-bye.

The amount of warmth generated in such simple encounters is incredible. A smile, a laugh, or a touch gave me passion for the people, for their culture, and for their country. It is amazing to think back on the time when I imagined China as an evil, Communist enemy. Last summer I developed special bonds in that country with some people whose names I never learned and with some people whose names I shall never forget. I discovered what wonderful, motivated people the Chinese are, and that they, too, valued friendship through communication as much as I do.

Name Withheld

For myself, living in Africa has given a commonplace quality to events that would be considered extraordinary in the United States. For example, at school pupils were occasionally assaulted by baboons, while in Nairobi bread and milk shortages were frequent. Similarly, on vacation from East Africa, there have been aspects of America's culture that seem alien and magnificent—

To me
The words
'Elizabethtown,
Lancaster County
Pennsylvania, U.S.A.'
mean two months every two years of reassuring luxury.

The immaculate green waves of corn form a secure wall
about the smooth macadam, as we drive in;
a sixty foot yellow 'M' to the left brings on a maniacal
craving
for a quarter pounder, and overweight women rock on their
porches
with a glass of iced tea, a bowl of pretzels.

The humid warmth feels relaxing the next morning;
in a T-shirt, a pair of slacks, and flip-flops, we walk up
the lane to the Hypermarket. Pure, white, neon-lighted
aisles;
things we dreamed of—watermelon and corn on the cob,
Grape Soda and pop tarts, bubblegum ice cream and Angel
Food Cake.

Staggering back beneath big brown packages, we look
at the trimmed hedges, spotless lawns; a polished Chevrolet
moves leisurely past, some kid floating behind it

on roller skates.

Later we sit wrapped in the reassuring and meaningless
colour of the television, absorbing 'The Price Is Right,'
our favourite game show, or Mork and Mindy. Of course,
        there's
a can of Mountain Dew balanced on our knees
while we chew a piece of Super Large, Grape Flavoured
                                Hubba Bubba Bubblegum.

Catherine Sustana

We always said we'd leave in the morning, but we could never wait. By four o'clock in the afternoon we were piled into the station wagon, Charlie McCoy playing on the stereo and the U-Haul humming behind us on the highway. We roared straight into the sunset, straight into our impatient adventure on I-40 West.

I couldn't sleep. This was tradition; I had to stay awake to see the Mississippi. The headlights, smooth and hypnotic, flashed by us in the opposite lane, growing thinner as the clock hands moved forward. The stereo had long since been turned off. My father was silent, and I watched my mother's head bob as she passed in and out of consciousness. I leaned forward and rested my chin against the front seat, staring into the black, foggy curves of the Smoky Mountains and waiting for the bridge.

When I woke up, the sun was pink and cool and flat. I looked out the windows and tried to imagine how far we had come. Oklahoma was flat and cool in the morning, like the sun. The tobacco farms had changed to ranches, and the sky had spread itself far into the corners of the horizon, but I couldn't escape the feeling that I could walk home, that there was no distance.

This is how every trip to the West began—a blind, passionate drive into Oklahoma ranches, Kansas wheat, Colorado mountains. We planned for weeks in advance, but the vacations always seemed spontaneous. This is where I first learned to trout fish, where I first saw beaver dams, where I first saw unexploited ghost towns. This is where we piled six people into a CJ-7 and bumped dangerously up Engineer Pass into the wilds of the Rockies, just the elk, the marmots, and the Sustanas. It was disorganized but heartfelt adventure.

The last time I visited the West I asked a friend what he wanted me to bring him. "Nothing," he said. "Don't bring me anything. Just write it all down, and remember it, and tell me everything."

I remember the way the clouds in New Mexico looked like a

window that had just been hit by a baseball. I remember the way the two boys in Magdalena, Arizona looked after they had wrecked their motorcycle. They were dusty and dazed, and I wondered why they were carrying so much beer on a Sunday morning. I remember the Chicano children in the IGA in Winslow. I remember the jewelry makers and the Indians and the trading posts and the fishermen and the ranchers and the blacksmiths and the gold mines.

This is what's important—to remember it, to write it down. I have stories, stories from every trip West, from every street festival, from everyone I have met, and from every day that the wind blows just right and the whole town smells like tobacco. Sometimes I can't remember crossing the bridge, but I get there, and I can write. Writing is my blind, passionate adventure, my communication that turns the curves in the dark and invariably crosses the bridge.

Essays About Obstacles

From the profound to the pitiful, how do you handle the problems that stand in your way?

The first two writers are inspiring in their strength and uplifting response to tough times. They describe wrenching, tragic circumstances without sinking into self-pity and pathos. With all they've been through, they should be able to deal with the transition to college without much problem. A difficult freshman course or a roommate with drums is unlikely to rattle them.

Jennifer Dodge, in her "Whomp!" essay, turns a broken leg and a potentially ruined year into an enlightening experience. She avoids syrupy glorifications of her charitable project and maintains a cheerful tone through the treacherous topics of pain and charity.

Christopher Harwood's essay on procrastination hit home with us (just ask our publisher). We identified with the writer while laughing with him, and the self-recognition made the humor even richer. The admissions officer who received this essay told us, "I chuckled with delight upon reading it, jumped up from my chair, and rushed into the hallway to share it with my colleagues."

Finally, effort can be more impressive than victory. Not only do most people avoid sorting out their personal conflicts in an application essay—they don't even try to sort them out in real life. In the last essay, someone is really trying, and that makes her impressive.

Laurie Jane Sternberg

One January night in the middle of my parents' three-year-long divorce proceedings, when I was fifteen, my father divorced me, just as he was divorcing my mother. He sat down with me and began to explain why he never wanted to speak to me again, unless I was willing to become the "loving" daughter that he wanted. He came to this dramatic and sudden decision because I was "too much like my mother" and because I had not acted "as he had hoped I would" during the divorce. I did not then and do not now understand my father's reasoning (I, after all, did not think my mother, with whom I lived, was so terrible) and his decision caused me great pain. But I did have to live with the reality of this decision and to deal, as a result, with both anger and frustration—his and mine.

My initial reaction was to alienate myself from my father and to give him the isolation that he seemed to be asking for. At the same time, I used the separation to assess the validity of his accusations. Was I in fact unloving? Was I cold? How did he want me to act? I finally decided that it was fruitless to dwell on the problem of how he wanted me to act. Instead, I had to act for myself. To my own surprise, I found also that I was not cold; I still loved him in spite of his harsh treatment, and I concluded that I could show him my love by working hard to mend our relationship so that both of us could be happy.

In the beginning, because I was so hurt and angry, I had to force myself to take the initiative. I called him nightly, carrying on one-sided conversations, although he rarely called me; I remembered birthdays and other occasions; I didn't pry into those things that he considered off-limits; I invited myself over to his home to spend time with him and to cook special meals for him; I asked him about his work. But I also tried to find other outlets for my anger into which I could channel my energy. Two of these, predictably, gave rise to further confrontations.

In my junior year of high school, I decided that I wanted to become an exchange student to Belgium, preferably for my entire senior year (admittedly, in part to escape from my angry father). However, my father believed that exchange programs were a waste of time and money (my mother's, not his), and that I would be better off taking tennis and golf lessons so that one day I could "catch a husband" by impressing him with my athletic skills. To him, exchange programs had no practical value.

His response made me very angry, but I needed his permission in order to go to Belgium. An angry shouting match would not have helped either of us; instead I tried patiently and calmly over a period of some weeks to convince him of the many rewards of the exchange experience. At the same time, I listened as openly as I could to his objections. We eventually reached a compromise, in which he permitted me to go abroad for the summer. Even more important, I gained his respect, along with his permission, and in addition, we both had the satisfaction of knowing that we could actually work through a difficult problem together. Our relationship really seemed to be improving.

My father also vehemently opposed my decision to work part-time during the school year at a local grocery store. He wanted me to "stop pushing myself" and to "take time off" and to save "work" for later in my life. I agreed with him that quitting my job would have obvious advantages, but I also knew that there were other advantages to working that, to me, outweighed the disadvantages. I enjoy the independence that comes with having my own income, small as it is. His lack of approval has made me angry, but I have listened to his objections, and we have again been able to reach a compromise. I have agreed to quit work at the first sign that I am pushing myself too hard or that my schoolwork is suffering. As a result, both his anger and mine have been effectively dissolved.

My dealing with my own anger has produced the unexpected benefit of helping my father to overcome his. We now have a good "relationship," if not exactly a marriage. I have learned to value Dad's opinion, through listening to him and discussing our differences openly. I have heard things that I often did not want to hear, and I have sometimes said things that I probably shouldn't have said. But I have also heard the truth, and spoken it, too. I have been forced to identify, understand, and eventually gain respect for another person's views, although they have often been completely opposed to my own. Instead of indulging myself in fits of temper, I have learned something about diplomacy. And in the bargain, I have shown to myself and to my father that I am in fact a loving daughter.

Alicia Jordan

Momma, Daddy, J.D., and Me

Try as I do I simply can not find a way to make the question, who has influenced greatly my personal development, light and humorous. The reason is my personal development has matured painfully, and though I am content with the person I am presently, it has taken many difficult incidents to mold me. The persons who have influenced my character the most through the last seventeen years are my father, my mother, and Jack Daniels. These three have definitely affected my life more radically than anyone outside of the immediate family could ever imagine. Perhaps this recount will at least partially explain it.

It was nearly dark when I finally got home from school. Dad had too many patients and consequently had been late picking up Laura and me that blistering cold Wednesday. I was eager to berate him when we got in the car, but I refrained since he looked exhausted with heavy brown eyes laden with frustration and irritation and that defeated grimace on his face that seemed to pervade his features perpetually of late. He seemed so lost, alone, and overwhelmed. I decided not to bother him. Instead, I just gave him a kiss and settled down into the warm bucket seat and enjoyed the sense of security which my father's presence assured.

We got home to a half-cooked casserole—Mama was not the greatest cook—and to one sister, Amy. Mama had taken Andrea, my five year old hyperactive sister, to children's church and presumably had gone to church choir as well. Dad threw out Mama's half-baked culinary effort and began again. Through necessity he had learned to putter around the kitchen with some skill and dexterity. The spaghetti he baked for us that night proved that. It was just what I needed. We ate, cleaned up, and went to our respective rooms to attend to our duties. About nine

40

o'clock a neighbor, Mrs. Carroll, brought Andrea home. "Lynne (mama) was nowhere to be found after church so I just went on and brought Andrea home myself," said Mrs. Carroll—she understood our family. She asked no questions.

We all began to wonder what had happened to Mama. It was not like her to be this irresponsible—something must have happened. Dad called all the hospitals, the family, and some friends. No one had heard from her. He decided to search for her. In the meantime I went back to struggling with Algebra Two. "Mama knows how to take care of herself," I kept thinking. Sure enough, about eleven thirty I heard her Suburban van sputtering up the hill. I turned off my light and went to sleep thinking that all was safe and sound. The next morning Dad told me Mama was still missing. I went to school that day a little worried, but well—after all "Mom does know how to take care of herself."

Thursday was another bitterly cold day—what made it significantly different was the feeling of bleakness and emptiness which not only invaded the outside atmosphere but also pervaded my entire outlook. I sensed the restlessness in the air, our house, and my whole existence. Little did I know it was the eve of my mourning.

I had to wait for Dad outside for forty-five minutes. When he finally picked me up about five thirty, I sensed something was wrong. He got out of the car and gave me a hug that almost crushed my frigid bones. All the while he mumbled, "She did the best that she could; she did the best that she could; she did the best that she could . . ."

"What's wrong?" I demanded—"Oh my God, I know, oh Jesus—no. It can't be true! Oh Daddy."

They had found her that morning. She held a pistol in the roof of her mouth with her right hand. With her left she gripped a bottle of Jack Daniels.

Mom's alcoholism and suicide caused me to mature at an accelerated rate. As my grandmother put it I am, "Seventeen going on twenty-five." I am the oldest of four siblings, and though my mother had many fine qualities and was not sick all of my life, her strong suits were not raising children, cooking, and housekeeping. All of these things she was persistently forced into doing because of her age, femininity, status, and location in the "old" South. When she became an alcoholic, partially in order to avoid those duties she detested, the jobs fell on Dad and me. Irresponsibility and childishness were out of the question. These things had to be done and there was simply no one else to do them!

Despite many of our "friends'" opinions, the situation was not completely distressful. Mom's illness helped to bring my father and me closer to one another than I think I will ever be to anyone else as long as I live. His wisdom, generosity, tenderness, and refusal to capitulate despite insurmountable odds gave me the strength to fight for all I believed in and dreamed for. He was and still is the mentor after which I have modeled my aspirations.

Also through reflecting on my mother's life, I feel as if I have become a better person. For instance, I understand more clearly now the importance of accepting one's own faults and the need to believe in oneself. Another of the characteristics which I developed prematurely is my independence. Mom was sick so much of the time that I often found myself fending all alone. I began arranging birthday parties for my sisters when I was fourteen, I learned how to grocery shop economically before I was thirteen, and I managed to organize and to cook dinners by the time I reached eleven. All of these skills I learned out of necessity have placed me "ahead of the game" now.

It might seem as if I have just finished recounting a miniseries of an afternoon soap opera, but these events and people are largely responsible for the person I am. Jack Daniels allowed my mother to ruin her life, but it also indirectly molded my personality. Coupled with my father's love, devotion, and wisdom and my mother's love, which she tried to express as well as she could, I have gained a type of courage and conviction in the path of many obstacles, but those difficulties provided much of my strength and vision.

Jennifer Dodge

It is tempting to describe myself to you in terms of grades, more lists of extracurricular activities, to expound on my love of reading, to, in fact, try to wow you with my attributes. But I'm uncomfortable with that, and you still wouldn't know any more about me as a person. I'm going to try to give you some insight into me by relating one experience and its ramifications.

My friends and I have a special word to perfectly describe an "ah hah experience". The word is Whomp! (You pronounce the wh as if you are saying what.) We use this word to describe what happens when something really hits you hard. For example: "I left my Accounting project at home, and, Whomp!, Mrs. Winslow gave me *six* extra assignments as a consequence!" Or, "I couldn't believe he took her out. Whomp! It's really over between us."

Okay. I hope you now have an idea of the significance of the word. With that as background I can tell you about the biggest Whomp! of my life. It happened early in October, 1984, during my junior year. I was with a group of friends at a cabin in the hills of Eastern Iowa. While standing on a balcony approximately thirty-five feet above the rocky terrain, the supports under the balcony gave way. Luckily for me, the ground broke my fall; unluckily, my leg did the same. One minute I was a healthy, mobile sixteen year old and, Whomp!, the next I had a leg in about fourteen different pieces, with some of those pieces protruding through a gaping wound.

My memories of the next few days are rather hazy. I can remember my mother's worried face hovering over me from time to time. I remember being told that I'd been through surgery and that they'd (the wondrous orthopedists) packed the bones together and fastened them at each end with pins. "Cool. You'll beep the airport metal detectors, Jen," my brother told me. Well, I'd also have sore armpits (crutches became my best friend and worst brother), and a cast up to my hip for six months. It seemed like an eternity.

Physical pain was the least of my worries. Whomp! People stared at me now. I couldn't take a shower. I couldn't go jogging. I couldn't stand for very long. I couldn't be on the track team. I couldn't get down to the newspaper room at school. I could watch TV—small compensation. I felt totally helpless and very frustrated at times. I needed help getting dressed, and getting to class, and getting into the car . . .

Wait a minute, this cast is only going to be on for six more months. Whomp! Some people are like this for their entire life. Some people have much worse problems that they must deal with every day of their existence with no light at the end of a six-month tunnel.

This really got me thinking. What would it be like to be physically handicapped? Dependent your whole life? These insights made me want to get involved. They made me want to do something to make a difference.

Now it's my senior year. Handicapped students (trainably mentally retarded kids, some with physical handicaps too) have been brought to Westside for their Special Education classes. I went to see the Department Head of Special Education. Together we devised a club called Peer Advocates which is like a buddy system between the regular education and special education kids. We have tried to pair the non-handicapped with the handicapped students according to interests and personalities. They are required to spend at least four hours a month with their match. We are also planning several group field trips to places like the zoo and bowling.

Organizing this group has been one of the most meaningful things I've ever done. Now kids of two totally different lifestyles are going out to lunch together and learning things about each other that they could never have learned from reading a book or studying handicaps. We are all learning compassion and tolerance and understanding. As for myself, I feel as though I'm doing something extremely worthwhile. For example, one morning, after a breakfast meeting of the group, a boy with Downs Syndrome named David walked up to me with a huge smile and gave me a great bear hug. He told me that he was so happy to have a special friend at Westside and thanked me. That was all I needed to know that the idea had been a good one.

44

Breaking my leg and its aftermath of pain and frustration was one experience I'd never want to go through again. But what it taught me was invaluable and I wouldn't change it for the world. It was a definite Whomp!

Christopher Harwood

There is a little demon that lurks in my conscious and unconscious mind that has done me more ill than any conventional ailment could. It is a stealthy creature that preys upon weakness and appetite and has ruined many a fair weekend in my life, and in the lives of many. The demon's name is procrastination, and he mocks me even as I type up the final draft of this essay. For the demon has triumphed again, and stolen my sleep, and he may triumph again after this. But I think not for a while, for this time he has stung me sorely, and my guard shall be up.

This autumn and winter have been a hectic time in my life, and the hectic time is when the demon thrives. In late October I began rehearsal for a play. The rehearsal schedule was not rigorous at first, and did not rule my life, but it was there. It was there and the demon seized upon it and assured me I had nothing to worry about; January and deadline time was still a long way off. And I was persuaded, and the further into rehearsal I went, the less I resisted the imp's devious advice. It was not long into rehearsal when the other, smaller deadlines began to creep up and rear their ugly heads, and paper after paper after test struck me unmercifully. And then the play was over. It was almost Christmas and now the responsibilities of shopping allied themselves with my academic obligations and thrashed me mercilessly while the demon chuckled, knowing that the real dealine was obscured and would be staggeringly painful to meet. Finally. Christmas was past, and the real deadline loomed ahead, frighteningly unobscured. Now the diabolical creature convulsed in unrestrained laughter, while I shuddered with a tinge of fear of imminent discomfort.

I then began the ordeal that would geometrically increase my misery daily until the Epiphany, when the deadline must be met. I cursed the demon, loudly at first, then more softly and then not at all. I stopped and I could only laugh an ironic laugh. For I realized that the demon does not exist; that he is merely an apparition that I have created. And discovering the power of creation I realized that I also have the power to dispell the creature. I know now that all I need do is seize the deadline in the distance and never shall the demon haunt me.

Name Withheld

Sometimes I think about all the things that have happened to me in my life and I wonder . . . what would the kids at school think if they knew that (Name)—straight A+(Name) the Brain whohastopgradesandherparentsneverbughersowhatmorecouldshewant– spent most of her childhood crying and feeling inferior because no one ever wanted to play with her or go to the mall or do normal kid things or be her friend and that the reason those grades were so important was that they were all she had? What would people say if they knew that my mom got divorced because she was a manic depressive and had to be hospitalized leaving little me and my baby sister in the care of Nana, who never liked Mommy and said mean things and made me cry into my pillow at night?

I remember when after living with her parents and getting better, Mom brought us home to be with her. I loved my special family. My grandparents weren't just faceless people in Florida who sent me presents every year. I thought things were perfect. I was very young then. In time I realized that Grandma and Grandpa were running the show, and although I loved them there were many things I didn't like about them: they were narrow-minded, hermitish, and they didn't trust Mom. I did, until she got sick in 1980. I felt scared and hurt by some of the things she said and did, and even after she got better it was a long time before I trusted her again. The whole situation began to improve when Mom started to date and to work part-time. I even hoped that we would be able to move out someday and be like a normal single-parent family.

(When I was sixteen, my dad, who was only forty-two but had high blood pressure and never went to the doctor no matter how much I cried, had a fatal stroke. Just when I was old enough to talk to him and get to know him as a person, I was cheated out of it, and I was mad as hell at him. I didn't even get to say goodbye.)

Nothing really changed, though. It was still Grandpa's house, and he was still in charge. I was angry at Mom for not standing up to him. Two years ago, Grandma got lung cancer. At first they didn't even tell me what it was. I don't know why I kept thinking she was getting better; I guess I didn't want to believe that Grandma would be gone so soon after Daddy. It wasn't until three months after the doctors gave up hope that Mom shouted at me "Don't you realize she's going to die?" and I did. The other unfair part was that Mom was finally ready to leave, and we couldn't. She said it would be different afterward. Grandpa would mellow and let her have more control. That was something I counted on when I was so stifled in the house that I could barely breathe, when my head pounded constantly and I ran out almost every night just to find some space to *be*.

Grandma died a few weeks ago, and for a couple of days sadness was eased by relief. Then Mom started to get sick, and our plans followed Grandpa's trust in her right out the window. I understand the immediate cause this time, so it doesn't hurt as much, but I still get angry and yell at her a lot. I guess I'm just feeling cheated, again.

I've written these things down for the first ever, and cried as I remembered some of them, and it seems hard to believe I've only been alive for seventeen years. Sometimes I get so sick of things happening to me that I want to scream (and many times I do). That's one reason I'm so anxious to get to college. I can't change my childhood into the one I wanted but next year I will be out on my own and I will finally have the chance to make my life turn out the way I plan it.

Offbeat Essays

These next essays are bizarre. From Oreos to flies to a friend named Sponge, the essays in this section use off-the-wall material to enliven the application and showcase the student's wit.

The playful mood and memorable images of David Bolognia's *My Nightly Ritual* are wonderful. Without getting repetitive, he explores all the possibilities of his topic, and he is smart enough to end the essay before the reader stops laughing.

Gail Lerner's funny essay on thumbsucking shows a lot of bravery—the revelation that she continues to suck her thumb at age eighteen is potentially embarrassing, after all. With a catchy, clever first paragraph, she pulls the reader into her essay and makes her story impossible to put down. You can bet admissions officers remembered her application.

Matt Weingarden's *An Untitled One-Act Musical* has one of the most original formats we have seen. It is a clever, confident applicant who can submit an essay like this, because, as a Yale English professor remarked, "Not many application writers have the nerve to rhyme 'accept' with 'adept,' or admit they have a friend named 'Sponge.' "

The "Move your ass!" essay is another very risky piece, but it works well. One admissions officer said, "I can't remember an essay in the past few months that has gotten so many genuine laughs. There is something about it that stops you dead in your tracks and makes you kick back for a minute and think about the entire process." (We should note that Barry Kaye wrote a longer, more serious piece for the second essay on his application.)

Joe Clifford's *Metaphor for Life*, a clever satire on the often pretentious "thought essays" (see later chapter) that students often submit, is just plain funny. Although Joe's philosophy may not appeal to everyone, his analysis of the word "the" stands above dispute.

Finally, Eve Berley concocted a humorous fantasy to satirize the admissions process. Her essay works, but barely. Though she shows a clever command of writing dialogue, she doesn't really say anything about herself. Fortunately, the rest of her application gave the admissions officer a good picture of her, so the essay was refreshing. But she was lucky.

Each essay in this section replies in a quirky, even flippant, tone to the question. The writer's wit becomes his selling point. But the offbeat essay can easily backfire. Admissions officers constantly warn that many "witty" essays are just not funny, and many often view them as inappropriate or even obnoxious.

Submitting an offbeat essay is a big gamble, but it can pay off handsomely if it's good. Our advice: let a lot of people read your offbeat essay before you send it, and make sure everyone else thinks it's as hilarious and ingenious as you do.

David Bolognia

My Nightly Ritual
(Heretofore Kept Secret)

The best thing to eat day or night, winter or summer,
anywhere in the world, at anytime, inside, outside, or upside
down, alone, or with a friend, is an Oreo cookie. I do not refer to
any Oreo cookie, but to the singularly succulent sustenance
which retains its number one position on the weekly top-forty
goody list, month after month. Of course, I refer to the
extremely palatable Doublestuff. Being a self-taught connoisseur
of this craft, I will share my experiences on exactly how to eat
these desirous, delectable delights.

First and foremost, I make extra sure Mom has them on her
shopping list weekly. Oreos without milk is like Laurel without
Hardy, so obviously, the second requirement is milk; it must be
cold and it must be fresh. The glass in which to pour the milk
must be short and fat, not tall and thin, for dunking purposes, of
course. If the preliminary steps have been completed and my
perspicacious dog has not discovered my intentions yet, it only
means more for me. (There are ways to trick even the wisest of
dogs, but let us not digress here.)

Once all the materials are gathered, I recline in a dimly lit
room and pig out. Taking one at a time so as to relish every bite
makes for a most memorable event. I never eat the whole cookie
right away because much can be told about a person by the way
he eats his Doublestuffs, and this method designates a boring
personality.

First, I turn the chocolate cookie part in a clockwise direction
and pull lightly, never pulling too hard so as to break it. I dunk
half the chocolate piece in the milk, eat it, and toss the
remaining half to appease the dog drooling on my leg. At this
point, depending on the mood and company, there are different
methods to follow. If time is short, I dunk the rest of the cookie,

52

quickly swirling it so as to soften it and plop the whole piece in my mouth. If I feel its weakening, the process is even quicker, because there is nothing worse than slugged milk. It is imperative to remember that a cookie in the mouth is worth two in the glass.

The classic style in Nabisco is the "bucky-beaver bite." It is done by scraping the front teeth down across the white cream paying particular attention to what is done so as not to bump the nose on the hard cookie. Once it is on my tongue, I fling my head back, swallowing it delicately. Of course, this method leaves another plain chocolate cookie, which the dog will gladly devour.

However, my all time favorite method of eating an Oreo is to build a bigger cookie; we have the technology. For this more complicated process, a butterknife is a necessity. The disassembling process is repeated. Now both chocolate sections must be removed from subsequent cookies. Here the butterknife comes in handy. This must be done gently so as not to break the cookie. The cream fillings are to be carefully stacked one on top of the other until guilt sets in or it no longer fits in the mouth. There is an option of eating the extra chocolates or gaining a life long friend in the now salivating dog. After admiring my creation, I "dunk-n-devour."

Lastly, every drop of milk is consumed while searching for drowning bits and pieces. Now I rinse the glass and take a follow-up swig of clean, fresh milk.

Following these easy instructions, even the most simpleminded person can become a creditable cookie consumer. Using any of these methods, I encourage everyone to partake in this epicurean delight. I am positive if all the men, women, and children of this world were to join in the sublime ritual of this art, we would have the happiest planet in the Milky Way. And now I feel this overwhelming urge to retire to the kitchen for more research.

Gail Lerner

When I was five, they told me that all my friends had stopped. I didn't stop. At ten, they told me that everyone would make fun of me. No one made fun of me. At fifteen, they told me that I was being silly. I still don't think it's silly.

I will concede that thumbsucking is not a particularly redeeming habit. It is, however, one of the best bad habits I know. At stressful times, some of my friends turn to assorted, sordid drugs, overeating, or the liberal abuse of loved ones. Others choose different orifices into which they jam their fingers. When in need of comfort, I simply pop digital tab A into oral slot B and become content immediately. It's discreet, subtle, and quietly rewarding. My teeth are still as straight as Chiclets.

My thumb and I did have our share of hard times. In first grade when my girlfriends abandoned their thumbs and turned to dreams of Shaun Cassidy, I alone remained loyal to my opposable sidekick. Now, when Shaun is but a distant memory, my thumb and I are still together. We have contemplated (and rejected) notions of hitchhiking, honed our thumb wrestling skills, and learned to write script together.

When my parents encouraged me to quit, I found a soulmate in Linus VanPelt of Charles Schultz's "Peanuts" comic strip. Compare Charlie Brown and Linus. Yes, good ol' Charlie Brown is the hero of the strip, but he is also five years old, bald, and already confined to Lucy's orange crate psychoanalysis. Linus, on the other hand, is an inventor and an artist. He sculpts delicate sand castles and paints elaborate imaginary murals. Armed with thumb and blanket, Linus is ready to face the world. He will never have a football pulled out from under him.

My nephew Max is a budding thumbsucker. When I read him his bedtime stories, I listen to this small, slurping creature beside me and watch him as he fingers the pages, transfixed by the story. No matter how much fun Max and I have running, chalk drawing, or building snow forts, I feel closest to him at bedtime when his thumb hangs precariously from his lower lip, anchored only by the forefinger curled around his nose. When I tuck him in, I think of all the potential he has and the choices he will be able to make. If the personal security offered by thumbsucking makes him feel more confident about his capabilities and enables him to make braver choices—all the better. If he does decide to stop sucking his thumb within the next few years, I will certainly support him in that decision as well. But I am looking forward to having another secret to share with him.

There are some surveys which insist that children who suck their thumbs beyond the age of six do so because they have not been sufficiently nurtured by their parents. These surveys are probably compiled by clinical, chainsmoking people who have never known the delights of a good book and a ready thumb. Children who continue to suck their thumbs do so because it is private, enjoyable, and relaxing.

There will always be naysayers, but I thumb my nose at them.

Matt Weingarden

An Untitled One-Act Musical

characters:
Matt, a Yale applicant
Sponge, his closest friend
a Chorus of their fellow high-school students

Scene: a Cranbook School corridor. Matt and Sponge sit against a wall; students walk by in both directions.

Matt: I've decided that I want to go to Yale. It's got everything I want—a good Classics department, a good English department, great science facilities—and from what I hear, it offers the best undergraduate education in the country. I'm not sure exactly what I'll major in—probably Classics or Classics and English—but it's important to me that the college I attend be strong in every area, because of my wide range of interests. I'll take a variety of courses: math, science, English, Latin, Greek, art, music. I want the best, most challenging education to be had, and I think I'll find it in New Haven.

Sponge: Fantastic. I hope you get in.

Chorus: (stopping abruptly in the hallway and singing to the tune of "When Johnny Comes Marching Home")
Oh, Matt is applying to Yale on his knees,
Accept! Accept!
Academically, socially, artistically, he's
Adept! Adept!
With his sharp sense of humor he knocks us all out,
He is a candidate we highly tout
And our song may be stale
But Matt ought to get into Yale. (students commence walking again)

56

Matt: Yeah, I hope I get in, too. I'm a little worried about it.

Sponge: Oh, I don't think you have anything to worry about. I mean, you're one of the best students in the school, you're involved in all those extracurriculars, you play guitar, you write, you draw and paint, you're an accomplished intramural athlete—what more could they want?

Chorus: (stopping again and singing to the tune of "My Bonnie Lies Over the Ocean")
While Matt prays for his Yale acceptance,
The Sponge thinks he's wasting his time,
Old Sponge says there will be no problem,
But Matt feels he need be sublime.
Take him, Take him,
We hope you decide to admit our Matt,
Take him, Take him,
We hope you accept our friend Matt. (they continue walking)

Matt: Don't be naive, Sponge. There are so many applicants that are more qualified than I am and the decisions are based on so many criteria—I just don't know.
(stands) C'mon. We'll be late for Physics.
(begins singing softly to the tune of "My Favorite Things")
Baseball and Latin, Frank Zappa and eating,
Science and drawing and writing and reading,
While playing at poker to be dealt four kings,
These are a few of my favorite things . . .
(Exeunt.)

Barry Kaye

(Question: What is the best piece of advice you've ever received?)

"Move your ass!" yelled a man as a car was bearing down on a five year old boy who was about to cross the street. That boy was me, and, needless to say, I took his advice and moved. As far as I'm concerned, that was the best piece of advice I've ever been given, for had I not received it, I would not be here today to say so.

The second best piece of advice I ever received was from my uncle, who said, "Barry, go to Medical School."

If I am not accepted to the University of Pennsylvania solely on the basis of this truthful answer, so be it. If I had not taken the man's advice, I would have gotten to Medical School anyway. As a cadaver.

Joe Clifford
_____

Metaphor for Life

Being so naive as to not have already developed a handy
metaphorical philosophy on life, I consider myself fortunate to
have stumbled upon one while watching television this weekend.
Our television is located in a "sun room"—a room dominated by
window space. Anyway, I heard a fly buzzing. It must have been
a healthy fly because it was January 4. The point is,
extraordinary health not withstanding, this was your typical,
stupid fly. That's because the fly proceeded to get himself stuck
in between a window and the venetian blind covering the
window. Ninety-nine percent of flies who enter our "sun room"
manage to place themselves in this compromising position. It's
actually quite sad. I can really sympathize with such a fly's
plight.

Anyway, after I killed this particular winter fly with a rolled-
up newspaper, I started thinking and this led to great
dividends—unerringly the result of any meditation that
originates due to observation of the insect world, a world that is
vastly underestimated by the general public. But I don't scoff at
the worth of insects and for this reason I decided to base my
philosophy on flies. Here it is: "We are, all of us, flies trapped
between the venetian blind and the window."

I suppose magnification of the ramifications of my philosophy
are in order. I think the best way to dissect my philosophy shall
be to examine it, word by word.

First "We." This means every human being on Earth, no
exceptions whatsoever.

"Are." The more observant will notice that this is a verb. The
truly elite will recognize this as a verb which links the
aforementioned pronoun to future modifiers.

"All of us," The commas here should clue you in. This is a handy grammatical trick that I used to emphasize the recently discussed universal scope of my deceivingly simple pronoun "We."

"Flies." Obviously, a key word. By saying "flies" I am transferring all the physical, mental and spiritual qualities of flydom onto humanity. This is a literary debt which I owe to Kafka with "Metaphorsis," Ionesco with "Rhinoceros" and Kurt Neumann, the director of the wondrous 1958 existential sci-fi movie "The Fly."

"Trapped." Another key word. It may refer to a claustrophobic helplessness in the human condition. It may refer to an absurd, no-way-out, Sisyphian nightmare or reality. It may also refer to Mel Tillis.

"Between." Relates closely to "trapped" and also "venetian blind" and "window." Seems to suggest that flies (AKA humanity) are in a hard place, so to speak. To cite a classical allusion—between Scylla and Charybdis.

"The." only an article. Nothing to get uptight about.

"Venetian blind." Caution. Heavy symbolism enters at this point. What a venetian blind is to a fly, so are clocks and watches to humans. Palpable time is a horrendous thing, something that erodes man to a powerless, devitalized shell.

"And." A conjunction.

"The." Once more, an article.

"Window." Again, be warned—deep symbolic commentary ahead. What a window is to a fly, so is realization of morality to a man. Already trapped on one side by clocks, man, like a fly, looks at the other alternative. The fly says "Oh no. There's a window. I'm doomed." Man says, "Oh no, There's my mortality. I better be extra careful." He sets restrictions and limits. He is trapped.

There you have my metaphorical philosophy. You may agree with me or you may think I'm a jerk. But ask yourself one question—"What time is it?"

Eve Berley

The Final Test

Stanley Albert Tukos waited patiently behind twenty-some-odd people. He felt confused, almost as if he had been hit over the head. After what seemed like an eternity, Stanley reached the front and approached the heavy-set woman behind the desk. He stood in awe at the huge gate which lay behind her. It was bigger than anything he had ever seen. "Name?" she asked.

"Where am I?" Stanley asked, dazed at what lay before him.

"Listen, mister," said the woman, "I don't have all day. What's your name?"

"Stanley, Stanley Tukos, but where am I and why do you want to know who I am?"

"What a'ya, stupid or somethin'? You're in heaven. Let's see, Tukos." She opened a book thicker than any dictionary Stanley had ever seen. "Ah, Stanley Albert Tukos, you were hit by a car, weren't you?"

"I don't know," said Stanley. "Am I dead?"

"I see we have a real Einstein here. Of course you're dead. What do you think this is, a joyride?" Just then two men approached the desk. Both were dressed in three-piece suits and, with the exception of their wings, looked more like Wall Street businessmen than angels in heaven.

"Mr. Tukos, we've been expecting you," said the taller of the two. "We understand you're probably a little confused as to your whereabouts but don't worry, that's normal. In time you'll understand where you are and what you're doing here. In the meantime, my name is Malcolm, and my friend here is Harvey. Malcolm is not my real name, but, well, that's a long story. Maybe one day I'll tell you about it."

"I don't want to hear it. I just want to go home."

"I'm afraid that's not possible. You see, we used to do that once in a while, y'know, send people back to earth, but it got kind of complicated. Some of them started remembering and appearing on TV shows like *Good Morning America*. They even made a couple of movies like, what was that one called, Harvey?''

''Beyond and Back,'' Harvey replied.

"Oh, yeah, well, it was bad publicity for us, so the Boss, who lives upstairs, kind of got upset."

"If this is heavan, said Stanley, "how come I didn't know I was dying?"

"It was very sudden," answered Malcolm.

"*Very* sudden, repeated Harvey, "and don't get too cocky, you're not in heaven yet. This is only Heaven's gate."

"Oh," said Stanley. "Well, when do I get to heaven?"

"We have to know a little more about you first," Malcolm answered, "Like why we would want you here in heaven. What have you accomplished?" Stanley began to grin.

"Well, sir, I invented the S.A.T."

"The who?" asked Harvey.

"The S.A.T., y'know. the Scholastic Aptitude Test. That's a very big deal back on earth. The test will either get a kid into college or keep him out. In other words, it separates the men from the boys."

"Y'know. I remember that test," said Harvey. "My son studied ten months for it and still ended up with a 1050."

"Oh," said Stanley. "I'm sorry to hear that. But think on the bright side, it's only his college education."

"You make a lot of kids very miserable, y'know. We don't like that attitude here in heaven. Did you do any Advanced Placement work during your lifetime?"

"What kind of work is that?" asked Stanley.

"Like charity, things that get you in good with the Boss."

"No, not really," replied Stanley, looking very disappointed.

"I don't know, Stan," said Malcolm, "we might have to reject you."

"Maybe not," said Harvey. "we'll see how you do on your Heaven Entrance Exam."

"Heaven Entrance Exam?" questioned Stanley. "That's not fair. I didn't have time to study. I didn't know I was going to die."

"That's all right, Stanley, you can't study for this. It's a piece of cake."

"But I didn't take the Kaplan course."

"Don't worry. you'll do fine. You can't study for this test," replied Malcolm. Stanley was then seated at a table and given a number of pencils. Three hours later, he finished and handed the test to Harvey. Harvey placed the exam in the computer and, in less than five minutes, returned with the results.

"Well, Stanley," says Harvey, "we have some good news and some bad news. The bad news is you got a 700 combined. The good news is we have a less competitive afterlife downstairs."

While You're Writing

1. Make sure you are answering the question appropriately.

2. Have a dictionary, a thesaurus, and a bottle of "white-out" handy.

3. Try different atmospheres. Write in silence, with music, at a baseball game, even during a boring math class.

4. If you get "writer's block," first try writing the whole essay the way you would say it. Or "talk" the essay into a tape recorder. Lastly, try stream-of-consciousness writing: write whatever you're thinking, and don't let your pencil leave the page for two minutes.

5. Let your essay sit for a few days, then reread it. You'll probably find a number of improvements you can make.

Self-Description Essays

All essays describe the applicant, but some do it more bluntly than others. Often the application asks you pointedly to "discuss yourself" or "tell more about yourself than your transcripts and scores already have." Stanford, for example, asked applicants to describe themselves using a "single adjective."

It's usually easy to write about yourself. High school students in particular are experiencing a wealth of self-revelation, so topics aren't hard to find. What's tough is making your writing interesting and memorable. After all, how many times do you think one poor admissions officer can read, "I've recently learned how important my friends are" or "After years of arguing, my parents and I are finally starting to develop a better relationship"?

The first two essays are for anybody who ever thought, "But I'm so ordinary. Nothing's ever happened to me worth writing about." Steven Branda makes an entertaining essay out of his ordinariness, and with subtle humor, he shows admissions officers that he's a funny, likable person, even though he proves he's "boring."

Daniel Burrows attacks the same problem, but in a different way. He shows that "average" people are vital to the success of any endeavor. One admissions officer said, "I suspect that few students could write an essay with this kind of skill and creativity. However, what most students can draw from it is how a single, striking image or series of analogies can have the impact that more formal prose can sometimes lack."

The third essay of this group, written by Dylan Tweney, describes a young man brimming with excitement and potential. "This essay blew me away, and still does," wrote an admissions officer at Williams College. "It offers such a direct view into the contradictions and complexities of a highly imaginative, creative, and complex person. It is both bold and sensitive, amazingly rich in imagery and unusual in structure. Dylan is a good bet to be a mold-breaker, an innovator." To anyone who doubts the importance of the application essay, imagine having that officer rooting for you in an admissions conference!

On Melinda Menzer's essay about telekinesis, ketchup soup, and searching for truth, an admissions officer said, "You have to believe that Melinda *will* make the tissue box move. She sweeps you away with the power of her ambition and positive thinking. Wouldn't you love to have her as a roommate?"

And Sarah Chinn doesn't tell you she's energetic and funny and insightful about her own limitations, she shows you through her attitude and her images. Her essay does the job admirably.

Don't be gimmicky. Do be creative, like Michael Meusey. In his quest for adjectives, he created a relaxed, playful essay. He seems to have had fun writing his piece, and that alone says a lot about his personality.

The final essay by Adam Ruben is a witty, insightful piece on a familiar high school ritual. By analyzing a commonplace occurrence in an unusual way, he displays a talent for wit with a curious mind. The essay is fun to read, and it said a lot about the Adam Ruben beneath his grades and test scores.

One last word of caution: When Stanford asked students to describe themselves in a single word, many applicants tried to be clever, writing "Concise" or "Brief" and leaving the rest of the page blank. Bad idea. It's not clever, it's definitely not original, and it really annoyed the admissions officers, who sincerely want to know more about you through your essay.

Steven M. Branda

The essay question sounds harmless enough: "Write about people who have influenced you, situations which have shaped you, difficulties or conflicts with which you have struggled, goals or hopes you have for the future, or something else you consider significant." I began to review the highlights of my life since my birth in Roseville, Minnesota: the year in Fort Leavenworth, Kansas, then moving back to Minnesota at the age of two, Thanksgiving Days spent dining in Golden Valley, summer fishing in Big Trout Lake, the exhilarating trip to see the Corn Palace in Mitchell, South Dakota, the spur-of-the-moment joy-ride to Darwin to see the world's biggest ball of string, the class field trip to the capitol building in St. Paul to see the world's tallest wooden Indian. Not much there to influence or shape a person.

Could my move to Shelburne, Vermont, be considered a difficulty or conflict with which I have struggled? Alas, I recalled how uneventful the transition to a new high school had been. Vermont students had failed to present me with challenges I could overcome and later write about. Extracurricular activities like dishwashing at the Shelburne Inn, lawnmowing and tennis in the summer, and the Champlain Valley Union High School Bowling Club looked even less promising.

I began to worry. Nothing seemed significant enough to be the subject of a College Essay; how could I honestly say that seeing the Corn Palace greatly influenced the course of my life? I needed something dramatic, something extraordinary. A hideous possibility lurked in the back of my mind: "Steve, . . . you're boring." At first I denied it, searching harder for really exciting episodes in my life. Gradually I became frantic, determined to prove to myself and to the rest of the world that I am not a boring person. In desperation, I turned to the people who know me best, individuals not afraid to stare me straight in the face and tell me the truth, and I put the question to them:

Richard Hood—"You're just another bleeding-heart liberal; you're a dime a dozen."
Joe Harvey—"You're about as boring as banana-carving, and I think we all know how boring that is."
Ian Wagner—"Boring? Hah! A fiend for an understatement, are you, Branda?"
Mr. Bob Peek—"Promise me you won't cry."

Now that reality confronts me, where does it leave my application? Colleges like Swarthmore try to select candidates who represent the whole spectrum of our diverse society, and I wholeheartedly agree with this practice. For all of the potential Heisman trophy candidates, the computer wizards, the seasoned world travellers, and the Big City sophisticates, there must be at least a few exceedingly boring applicants accepted, if only to provide balance. Swarthmore needs me for diversity. My goal, of course, is to become a more interesting person; that's why I need Swarthmore.

Daniel Burrows

Who is Daniel Burrows? Good question.

I am a familiar person, one that you have certainly seen before. I am an old acquaintance who I'm sure you know quite well. You see, when all is said and done and everyone has gone home to sleep, I stand there alone; noble and unnoticed. I observe it all. I am the hero's best friend.

It seems that it has always been my part in life to be the second man on the moon or the guy who blocked for O.J. Simpson. I'm not complaining though. My job is very important and in many ways, much more difficult. I have to be brilliantly consistent without ever being obtrusive. For example: I'm the blond-haired kid who gets hit by a ricochet just as the army is about to go over the top. My dying words are "tell my mother I fought bravely". I'm just a sweet, simple kid who doesn't deserve to die in absolutely every war movie you have ever seen. It's the kind of consistency that requires a very light hand; *anyone* could be John Wayne.

In a world of "stars", "co-stars" and "special guest stars," I'm a "with"; but I always remember my lines and play my character to its fullest. All I ask is that you be patient and attentive, allow me to make you laugh or cry. Let me do this and we will both be happy. I guarantee it.

I'm the person who places the parsley on your $17.50 Veal Oscar. I never used too much or too little and my little piece of parsley adds style, grace and beauty to your dining experience. Without my parsley you would detect a vital missing ingredient but would be hard pressed to figure out exactly what it is. You'd inspect the wine and perhaps lightly pepper your food, yet something would be missing. Everyone needs a little parsley.

Finally, I'm that third person singular narrator that you've been wondering about all these years. For as long as you've been reading books, you've been wondering who the omniscient observer is. We are one in the same. I know all, and what I don't know I can find out or, best of all, make up. I can wield my imagination as a sword or a feather; sometimes both.

I like being the hero's best friend even if it does occasionally mean being Andrew Jackson's horse or the Habsburg's butler. Though you may not remember my name, you will never forget me. You will miss me when I have gone.

Dylan Tweney

I am:

Blinded by science, saved by Zero, thrown from a fairy tale, across the pit of what could be, and back into the magic again, smoking with restrained passion and still shivering from the bitter winds that blow through my skeleton, which I left behind for awhile when I decided that I was a magic soul trapped in a mechanistic body.

The funniest thing is that my skeleton does just as well by itself as it did when fleshed and blooded and clothed. No one has noticed that my devotion and greatest concentration are no longer on my schoolwork, even while that bare skeleton of attention is beginning to crumble.

I am:

Old like Kronos, young as the dew, day-to-day variable like the wind, now a soaring dove far above the petty concerns of familial and social life, now an irascible, excitable bear in a box. Obviously egotistical as hell. I've always been plagued with fantasies of greatness. They're fine, but at one time they were the only fantasies I had. Eager to be the greatest scientist the world had ever known, I devoted myself to my studies and launched myself into the sea I thought I belonged in, because I had known no other since falling in love with school at the age of five. I've since re-emerged from that surf, foam on my mouth.

But to many I seem stable, calm, rational, "boring." They may be right. It's possible that I'm suffering from delusions of artistic grandeur, or that I'm simply trying to make myself feel better by pretending to be of a romantic cut. Or it may be that I actually am a turbulent person with a calm exterior deriving from a strong sense of self-control and modesty. I can truly let go to create and to communicate only in art (but what a term— "art"—it sounds like some kind of prostitution). So my soft artist's body: blood, brain, intestines and all, has gone on to paint, draw, write (and sing surreptitiously—and quite poorly—in the closet), while my bones remain behind to prop up a convenient image back in school.

I am also:

Obsessed. The hormonal soup and budding sexual instinct present in every seventeen-year-old boy happened to swirl up into the head of one whose patience, dedication, faithfulness, and general stupidity amaze even himself. That is to say (with all the irony due such a bizarre Junior year): I spent almost an entire year and a half waiting, admiring, and damn near privately worshipping a young lady with whom I was desperately infatuated; by the time she came around last summer and decided that she was crazy about me, too, it was two weeks before she had to leave for Germany as an exchange student—meaning I have to wait another year, for no certain return. But, I love her, quite sincerely, and my feeling is that most people really love only a few times in their lives, so I'm not giving up on this one, not yet, not just because over five thousand miles and thirty million seconds separate us.

I am:

Emerging from this essay intact, shaking off the beads of fancy and words and metaphor, hair dripping with sweat from the exertion of the usual Olympian attempt to create (100% self) and communicate (half self and half audience), yielding one more work with the ideal ratio of 3 me : 1 you. Another four-part structure! If I'm done writing, you're done reading me. Do you feel you know me any better?

"Life is serious but art is fun."—John Irving

Melinda Menzer

Sometimes I sit in my room and try to move things. I stare as hard as I can at, say, a tissue box and think, "MOVE!" Crinkling up my forehead, scrunching up my eyes, I will with all might that the tissue box will levitate. So far, nothing has ever moved. But I am still hoping to develop extra-sensory powers.

I guess what I fear most is being ordinary. Well, let me qualify that. I fear nuclear holocaust, robbers under the bed, big, furry tarantulas, and the theft of my dear teddy bear, Phoebe, just as much or more. But I don't want to be ordinary. Ordinary is boring; ordinary is pointless; ordinary is so very . . . ordinary. Anyone can be ordinary. But I don't want to be just anyone.

Reading *Crime and Punishment* made me think about being ordinary. Raskolnikov, the main character, wants to prove that he is extraordinary, that he is a super-man. To do this, he kills a woman pawnbroker. Now, I don't need to kill anybody; I am a tad more laid back than Raskolnikov. But I, too, want to do something. I have a predilection towards living in a garret, eating ketchup soup and Saltines, writing The Great American Novel. Or, like Larry Darrell in *The Razor's Edge*, I could travel the world in search of truth, doing good "for the love of a God he doesn't believe In." I want to sacrifice for a worthy cause; I want to change the world; I want to make the difference.

Now, they tell me I'm a pretty smart cookie. I have the credentials: good SAT scores, National Merit Semifinalist, four AP classes. As cookies go, I'm near the top of the jar. But am I a boring, bland, sugar cookie or an ordinary, carbon copy, buy-at-the-supermarket cookie? Or am I a super-duper, slightly eccentric, rough but delicious, homemade, one-of-a-kind oatmeal-raisin cookie? I refuse to be just another ordinary cookie in the crowd. Eventually I'll win the Nobel Prize for Literature, or I'll discover the nature of genetic processes. Perhaps tomorrow will be the day I make the tissue box move.

Sarah Chinn

Most people are afraid of what will happen on Judgement Day, but I don't have to worry about it. I'll walk into a room, my karma floating gently before me, arguing with my eternal soul about who should go in front, and a great voice will boom:

"Will the real Sarah Chinn please stand up!" And there I shall be, facing the void between heaven and hell (purgatory is not a Jewish fear; we work off our guilt on Earth) not knowing where to put myself. Let me explain.

I am a "little bundle of contradictions." I live my life between the one hand and the other, weighing up the odds and waiting for it to come out even. I am happy to be alive, joyous, outgoing, loving and lovable. On the other hand, I am sometimes deeply depressed, afraid, shy, hating and hateful, disillusioned with the world as it is and wishing how it might be. I am a city girl: I love noise, buildings, even dirt, and the never ending grimy rain. But there is a freedom in endless miles of green field that draws my head away from the grubby claustrophobia of New York City and its concrete mile-high gravestones, stretching out into one enormous mausoleum. I am typical prim English, the product of a girls' school education: dogmatic, self-assured, liberated but restrained. And then I am the American High School Senior: wild, laughing at fast cars and football games, madly applying to college, going out to parties and burning the candle at both ends, never fearing the dripping wax as it gets nearer and nearer the middle.

You're right, scores and grades can tell you very little about a person, although it is difficult to sum up "everything-about-you-we-don't-already-know-but-you-think-is-interesting" in such a small space. I am glad that Yale is not the Eternal Judge, although at the moment it feels that way. But the real Sarah Chinn . . . ? The real Sarah Chinn loves her life, loves her inconsistencies, loves to make people wonder what she will do next. She is a little radical in her politics, a little hypocritical in her actions. She is trying to change the world and trying to stop it from changing her too much.

Michael Meusey

I would like to take this opportunity to discuss the experience I had filling out this application. In particular, I will focus on the section which asks for three adjectives to describe oneself. I found this to be a somewhat difficult task, having to sum myself up in three words. In this essay I will relate to you the trials and tribulations of my attempt to do so.

At first it seemed this would be the easiest part of the application. When I first read it the three words that immediately came to mind to describe myself perfectly were: tall, dark and handsome. However, when I sprung this idea on my girlfriend I began to have second thoughts. First of all she said that I wasn't really tall, just above average in height. Also, the only time I could be considered dark was at the height of my summer tan, and even that was stretching it. Finally, she didn't know if she would go so far as handsome, but she did say that I was not ugly. At that point I decided to revise my choices since "above average height, occasionally dark, and not ugly" wasn't exactly the image I wanted to give.

I was then struck by a new inspiration. I could use words that were very vague and able to be interpreted in several different ways. I thought of such words as "talented", determined", and "motivated." I figured I was home free since these words would make me sound good and I wouldn't have to say where my talent, determination and motivation lie, it would just be assumed I was referring to academics. As I went to type them onto the application form, the pat on the back I was giving myself became a slap in the face when I discovered I had to explain why I had chosen those words. So much for that idea.

My next approach was to portray myself as an academic wonder with such words as: studious, scholarly and intellectual. This time, it was my conscience that made me decide against these words. I felt they would get your hopes up too high in expecting a horn rim wearing, sliderule-toting genius destined to bring fame to the university with my academic prowess. While those adjectives are accurate to a point, they are sometimes overridden by such words as: rebellious, lazy and mischievous. I considered using these as a warning to you, but like their predecessors they seemed to over-emphasize one side of my personality while neglecting the other.

Next I decided to use a humorous approach. I tried using adjectives with radically conflicting meanings. After much thought, I settled on "brilliant", "gorgeous" and "modest." However, I could find no feasible way of explaining such a combination, so I was forced to abandon yet another idea.

Becoming somewhat frustrated, I decided to take a more liberal interpretation of the question. After all, there was nothing in the instructions that said the adjectives couldn't be made up! So I invented the words "semiomniscient" and "quasiomnipotent", but couldn't think of a third. Undaunted, I further liberalized my interpretation of the question by realizing that the words did not have to be in English, so I made up a word in German to complete my list. I came up with "ricebildperfekte" which, loosely translated, means "picture-perfect for admission to Rice."

At this point I realized that this ploy, though clever, would not quite make it. Glancing at the clock and realizing that I had been at this for several hours, I became so distraught that the only adjectives that came to mind were ones such as these: frustrated, exasperated, defeated, tired and hungry. But after a sandwich and a quick nap, I was refreshed and had a new plan. All I had to do was come up with three basic adjectives that describe me and then look them up in a thesaurus to find more glamorous sounding synonyms. Thus in no time at all "friendly, honest, and hard-working" became "amicable, veracious, and assiduous." But before I could type them up, I began to wonder: could this candy-coated version of the truth be a violation to the Rice Honor System? Not wanting to take the chance, I gave up on this idea too.

This was my darkest moment. Though I was determined to work at this until I found three adjectives, I had already come up with several different ideas, though not one of them was workable. However, I still felt that I could resolve this problem. Then suddenly I realized that all of this had in itself brought out three of my most important personality traits—perseverance, creativity, and optimism. I utilize these traits in solving any problem, including those in school. Optimism gives me enough confidence in my abilities, and perseverance and creativity work together to allow me to try all possible methods of solving the problem without giving up. In this case, confident that I could eventually come up with the three adjectives, I tried several different methods of selecting them and finally arrived at what I feel to be the most representative of myself. Thus ends my long and frustrating quest for the three elusive adjectives. Now, if I could just figure out which book or movie to write about . . .

Adam Ruben

"The devil can cite Scripture for his purpose."

Such was my attitude as I began the quest upon which all high school students must eventually embark: the search for the perfect phrase to summarize their life to yearbook readers now and twenty years hence. Essentially, a yearbook quotation has to represent "you". It can be a summary of your views on life, liberty, and the pursuit of eggnog (it's difficult to find anyone quotable whose views on the subject coincide with mine); it can be a tribute to the unique and lasting friendships formed in high school (this category of permissibly sappy quotations is best gleaned from popular songs and movies); it can be a sample of writing noteworthy for its unique style (Tom Robbins on Diane Keaton: "A smile that could paint Liberace's ceiling, butter a blind man's waffles, and slush the accumulated frosts of Finland Station.") or for its source (an eighth grade teacher, after learning my name two months into the course: "You can't fool me anymore. I know who you are."); finally, and often most attractively, it can be an irrelevant statement, funny in a reserved sort of way (to wit, Emerson's "Beware of endeavors which require new clothes."). The more of these requirements an individual quotation satisfies, the better.

Thus I set forth on *Yearbook IV, The Search for Schlock*. No, not all yearbook quotations are schlock (though many are stock or designed to shock); actually, when I sat down to choose several quotations for my yearbook page, I realized how trite many quotations were, and was prompted to compile a Lettermanesque list of the Top Ten Most Overused Yearbook Quotations (headed by "Anything by Billy Joel") for the school newspaper. I originally felt a need to unearth the one quotation in the world that perfectly described me, in terms of my philosophy, my wit (which I always seem to appreciate more than anyone else), my attitude toward friends, and of course, my views on life, liberty, and the pursuit of eggnog. I realized, however, that the chances of stumbling across such a quotation were rather slim. I tried then to find a quotation encapsulating each element of the strange compound that is me.

I found a great quotation to describe my philosophy while reading a recent issue of *Esquire* magazine (an obsession of mine); unfortunately, the epithet is Bob Dylan's, and I am reluctant to print his name on my yearbook page lest anyone (including myself at some distant reunion) think I like his music. Nevertheless, the quotation is apt: "Well, you always know who you are. I just don't know who I'm gonna become." I find it comforting to know that as I sit pondering the course of my future and my past (for the benefit of admissions officers unbeknownst to me), someone can elucidate my thoughts better than I, even if it is Bob Dylan. Alternatively, Shakespeare's words please me: "The man that hath no music in himself . . . Is fit for treasons, strategems, and spoils." Like me, the words are a little dramatic, a little offbeat.

My wit, too, is somewhat skewed, a fact which provides me with frequent pride and frequent humiliation, but rarely embarrassment. In this arena I look to a man who is certainly as strange as I, if much funnier and better paid, Woody Allen. One of his best lines explains that, "The true test of maturity is not how old you are, but how you react to awakening in the midtown area in your shorts." Also, Steve Martin exhorts musically, "Be obsequious, purple and clairvoyant,/Be pompous, obese, and eat cactus,/Criticize things you don't know about,/Be oblong and have your knees removed." My kind of guy. I cannot resist one more, so brilliant it puts the strings of puns I trade with my friends to shame: When asked to use the word "horticulture" in a sentence, Dorothy Parker responded, "You can lead a horticulture, but you cannot make her think."

As for my friends, finding the right quotation is crucial. I take my friends very seriously, which is more than they can say about me, so I'll allow myself a serious quotation (preceded by an anonymous "Life is just one big in joke to you guys, isn't it?") courtesy of Bruce Springsteen, sans grammaire: "There ain't nobody, nowhere, nohow gonna ever understand me the way you did."

Finally, I can only approximate my views on life, liberty and the pursuit of eggnog with a collection of a few quotations: from *A Midsummer Night's Dream*, "Things do best please me/That befall prepost'rously;" from *Where the Wild Things Are*, "Let the wild rumpus start!"; and finally an unattributed tribute to the wondrous world we live in, "And the eggnog isn't even sour yet!"

Essays About Home

We've spoken with many applicants who say they were a little depressed after reading the essays in our book. Sure, they say, they could write a good essay, too—if they had lived in China or had organized some big, successful charity program. But, they whine, all they've ever done is work as a cashier at the Qwik Stop or as a lifeguard at the local pool. How exciting is that?

Not very. You'd have to be a gifted writer indeed to make the Qwik Stop seem thrilling and adventurous. (We know—we were both cashiers in high school.) But there are interesting and amusing things going on all around you, especially at home. If your family is anything like ours, you should be able to find plenty of material just by looking around you. Even your boring old hometown offers great essay material if you look at it from a new perspective.

Erin Miller, for instance, lives in Round Pond, Maine. Population: "300 people, 49 cats, 32 dogs, 6 moose, 2 pigs, 1 llama and 493,000 lobsters." Though Round Pond is just a sleepy little town, Erin finds so much color and charm that you can't help but chuckle, and the comparisons she makes between Round Pond and New York City are wonderful.

Ryan Riggs takes his hometown of Memphis and defends it against the "Elvis-ville" stereotype we all have. You have to admire his energy as he defends his city's reputation and integrity.

Maeve O'Connor's beautiful essay about remembering her deceased father is perhaps the warmest, most personal essay in the book. She opens herself up to the reader and invites us into her family. We feel the pain and the loss with her, but even with the sadness, she manages to keep the tone optimistic and strong. It's an extraordinary piece of writing.

Sterry Butcher's essay about Bessie, Oklahoma, is a lot like Erin Miller's, but much grimmer. She, too, paints a vivid picture of the people and life of her small town.

And even if your homelife isn't idyllic, you still should consider it as a potential essay topic. Jennifer Don's essay about life in an institution certainly isn't sweet and happy, but admissions officers don't want sweet and happy applicants. They want honest applicants. Since the institution was a major factor in shaping Jennifer's outlook, it's definitely an appropriate essay topic. The truthfulness and emotion in her piece gave admissions officers insight into her character and her development—and that's exactly the purpose of the essay.

In the last essay, Isaiah Cox weaves a fascinating, memorable tale about his up-bringing. If you think your home life is dull, imagine growing up in "the Middle of Nowhere, Idaho"—and then study how effectively Isaiah writes about it.

Erin Miller

The most significant "experience" of my life has been that I have grown up in diverse environments. My parents divorced when I was two years old and since then, I have lived in the extremes of Round Pond, Maine and New York City. Traveling between my two very different homes has given me a stranger view of the world than I would have developed living in just one culture or community. I have seen the best and the worst of both extremes and learned to appreciate them without taking either too seriously.

Round Pond, Maine has a population of about 300 people, 49 cats, 32 dogs, 6 moose, 2 pigs, 1 llama and 493,000 lobsters. It is one of five villages making up the town of Bristol, which lies on the western shore of Muscongus Bay, in Lincoln County. One might expect to find, in the village of Round Pond (logically), a "round pond", but this is not the case. The "pond" is a harbor and the harbor isn't particularly round.

The population of Manhattan is about six times greater than that of the whole state of Maine, but people refer to Manhattan as an island. Technically, I suppose this is correct. However, my concept of "island" derives from the numerous rocky ledges lying off Round Pond Harbor. Hogs Head Island or Upper Goose Island, for instance. Islands are remote. Manhattan Island is anything but remote.

Walking down Main Street (in fact the only street) in Round Pond, one will note that practically every mailbox bears the names Hanna, Poland, or Leeman. One can receive mail bearing only a surname and a zip code. Georgia Leeman, the post-mistress, knows everyone. In New York, most of my father's important mail gets lost, and the only letters that do arrive are addressed to someone else.

I find the basic attitudes of each culture very curious. My mother refuses to buy a clothes dryer because "it is an unnecessary waste of electricity." It is not uncommon to see her wearing snowshoes to hang out clothes to "dry". Four feet of snow won't stop her. The clothes freeze solid until you put them on, then they proceed to melt. Wearing wet clothes in winter is not comfortable. This story is amazing to most New Yorkers, where conservation of electricity is not very prevalent. Why are those millions of lights left on all night? And in a power outage, New Yorkers panic. Time stops; no one does anything. No one can understand why the television doesn't work. In Maine, we just get out the kerosene lanterns and read. Round Pond remains one of America's few cable-less villages. Residents don't have their MTV, and probably never will.

The primary social event of Round Pond is the annual 4th of July parade, which began in 1986. Organized by its founders as a small gathering of friends, the event has become a major attraction. The parade is usually longer than the town. The rear of the procession watches the front of the procession until it is time to march. Upon finishing, the front of the procession returns to watch the rear of the procession. This concept evolved with the realization that everyone in town was participating and that there were no spectators. The favorite parade of most New Yorkers is the Macy's Thanksgiving Day procession. What amazes me is the number of people who turn out the night before to watch the inflation of the large balloons. This has become a major event. People stand for hours in the frigid night, deriving strange pleasure from watching helium being pumped into plastic.

In 1966, Round Pond had the distinction of becoming the first town in Maine to witness the burning of its own fire station. This unfortunate accident was blamed on the explosion of an electric toilet. Town residents made the best of the incident, picnicking on the nearby church lawn while watching the blaze. The unprepared volunteer fire department was unable to extinguish the flames. Four hundred and fifty miles to the south, the excellently equipped and trained New York Fire Department sits in traffic while obnoxious cab drivers refuse to move. In both places, the fires burn and the people watch.

Though Round Pond is in a remote part of the world, important international events have occurred. In 1988, Round Ponders fraternized with Russian seamen during a volleyball game on board a Soviet Pogie (a fish used for bait) processing ship anchored just off shore. It is known that the Russians didn't stand a chance against the strong Round Pond team. In New

York, a single Russian recently managed to shut down the entire city. Six years after President Reagan called the USSR "an evil empire", New Yorkers lined the streets chanting "Gorby! Gorby!". Round Ponders consider themselves to have set the stage for this international development.

Ryan Riggs

Misconceptions—I hate them. Although they will always exist, I will still fight my private little war against them and especially against one that concerns me directly. During my travels in the summer, I always meet interesting people and attempt to make new friends. However, one common bond ties all of these strangers together: fallacious thoughts about my city. The conversation usually begins innocently enough:

"Hi, my name's Ryan Riggs, how are you?"

"Fine. So, where are you from?"

"Memphis."

"Memphis, Tennessee?"

"Yes, Memphis."

"Wow! Do you go see Elvis' house all the time and own all of his albums? I read about you guys in *USA Today* this summer—sounds like a blast being with Elvis!"

Boom. That's when it hits—the most common mistake about my life and my city. When non-Memphians think of Memphis, only one thought flashes into their brain: the hometown of The King of Rock and Roll, Elvis Presley. Because I live in Memphis, many non-Memphians think that I ardently admire Him and always attend the annual candlelight vigil near his gravesite on August 23, the anniversary of his death. They also think that I own all of his albums and seem confused that I do not have thick, black sideburns and well-oiled hair. So that you, too, do not get the wrong idea, let me set the record straight.

Yes, I do live in Memphis. Yes, Elvis lived here, too. No, I do not make annual pilgrimages to his house or buy "Love Me Tender" shampoo. I have seen Elvis' house only twice in my life, both times to appease out-of-town guests. My latest trek down Elvis Presley Boulevard occurred not long ago when a buddy whom I met while at Boys' State came to visit. Upon arrival at the mansion, I cringed at the $6.50 admission fee, but capitulated when I learned that the Elvis movie was included in this special off-season price. As our tour guides herded us through the vast assortment of rooms at Graceland, I admired Elvis' exquisite taste and pragmatic decor: A 24-carat gold piano, the "jungle room," and the "entertainment room," with five color televisions and two stereos. Lastly, I paid my final respects to The King in the "Meditation Gardens," where he and his family are laid to rest. Several other tourists wept, but I suppressed my emotion and calmly strolled back to the tour bus.

I hope that you now understand why I resent the automatic association of Memphis with Elvis. I might sound cynical towards a man who has bolstered my city's economy so much, but I have a right to sound that way. Many worshippers of The King tend to skip over the details of his life. His first albums (some of which I do have) are masterpieces, but from there his music and his life steadily decline. The Tour guides at Graceland will not tell you that Elvis' heart failure was brought on by a massive drug overdose. That is my frustration with Elvis. The man had everything but threw it all away.

The story of Elvis taught me a lesson, though. Now, as I strive for success, I know how *not* to use any achievements that I may obtain. Elvis is a classic example of a man who was ruined by fame and fortune, and I am determined, if I ever gain prosperity, not to let it ruin me. So whenever I meet non-Memphians I do my best to convince them that although I live in Memphis, I do not follow that cult of Elvis worshippers who account for three-fourths of all the tourists in Memphis. I refuse to allow Elvis Presley's specter to dominate the perceptions and misconceptions about my city. Of course, I realize the impossibility of convincing two-hundred and forty million other Americans of the ridiculousness of this myth, but many non-Memphians will always remember me as the guy who debunked The King.

Maeve O'Connor

Last Thursday was my father's birthday. I was standing on the sideline at my soccer game, shivering in the cold October drizzle, when suddenly I remembered. He would have been 53.

When I got home that day, Mom was in her room, sorting through some of my father's old sketch books. She had remembered too. I told her I thought we should spend the evening doing something Dad would have liked to do, and she smiled and said that was a wonderful idea. We selected a symphony by Beethoven from the stacks of records in the music room, and then the five of us gathered close around the small kitchen table for dinner. We ate by candlelight, laughing as we remembered.

No one had made a birthday cake, so when we had finished we went to Brigham's for ice cream. My father had loved to take us there on special occasions. I would have liked a dish of mocha almond, but I ordered chocolate chip with jimmies, just like I used to every time Dad took us to Brigham's when I was small.

It's cold out today, and I'm wearing my father's Irish sweater. He used to wear this sweater all the time on winter weekends. It has big holes in the shoulders that he never bothered to sew, but it's thick and warm, and our old house is drafty. In the past year or so, one of the holes has stretched so far that I'm afraid the entire sleeve will come off, but I don't want to mend it. I love the holes.

Sterry Butcher

Bessie is a tiny town in the wheat plains of Oklahoma. I am close to this place, to the eggshell colored grain elevators, the Hereford cattle, and my Grandmother who lives there. She lives in a tall, white clapboard house with a kitchen out back. Bessie is too small now for an elementary school, the school age children are bussed to Cordell, but the old school house is now used as a center for rehabilitating Arapahos.

Most of the residents of Bessie are either elderly, on a fixed monthly income, or oil field roughnecks whose job security is, at best, tenuous. Many are on welfare. Blue, pink, and white mobile homes cluster on the horizon like guinea hens, a strange juxtaposition to the fertile wheat fields that surround them.

Bessie has its own personality, though, a quality that is sometimes difficult to find in larger cities. There is a motorcycle gang who live in an old, red brick building downtown. Mrs. Crane is convinced they are dope runners. To the surprise of everyone in town, they had a Christmas tree this year, a blue Christmas tree.

There is Oscar, who has the largest nose and oldest overalls in three counties. He gives me a quarter each time he sees me. "How's that granddaughter of your'n?" he periodically asks my Grandmother. Oscar can't read or write anything but his name. Each month Grandmother has his Social Security check filled out and deposited for him.

Jane lives in the tan trailer in the abandoned cotton field west of town. Agnes Crouse thinks Jane looks just like Elizabeth Taylor. Sometimes Jane will bring her two kids to Grandmother's house to watch "Wheel of Fortune" on television. "Virginia," she'll say, "Please feed these kids a decent meal."

There is, of course, my Grandmother. A few years ago, she quit her cashier job at Humpty Dumpty Supermarket in Cordell to become mayor of Bessie. Recently, she has given that up too, in order to take care of her garden and to keep a closer eye on her mother. Grandmother Nealie, my great grandmother, has claimed to be ninety-nine years old for the past two years. She is superstitious and believes it bad luck to ever reach one hundred. Mornings, they can be seen, early, feeding the stray cats and tending tomato plants.

I wonder, though, how all these people will fare during the next four years. The Reagan Administration has proposed to cut funds that would mean the closing of the Indian Rehabilitation Center. During his first term, the President directed a commission to find out if there was hunger in America. Their study showed that there was none. Yet I know there is, at least in one small town in Oklahoma. I am worried about the possibility of Reagan cutting the Social Security and welfare that keeps some people of Bessie from blowing away in a cloud of red dirt. And I am frightened of the consequences of the freezing of Medicare payments, an action that would overburden millions of people, including some I know.

Jennifer Don

Perhaps we were children of a lesser God. There was definitely some understood though unspoken connection between us—an innate bond which united us fledglings in our lonely nest from which we viewed the world together. We were children on the fourth floor, and behind our barred windows and locked doors we trod in silent single files and followed the same routine from day to day, watching the seasons turn without us. We ate and slept and studied and played together, and watched appropriate movies twice a month and danced to appropriate music on special occasions. All this is fact, but there was much more to it. This separate world was a haven to us—a veritable shelter where we, the sheep who had gone astray, sought the depths of our truths and of ourselves. One way or another we had all gone too far, seen too much, aged too soon. As flowers which bloomed before their springs, we had felt the biting frost; thus we were, more or less, there for the same reason—because we were hurt. Pain held us and our innocence in its chains and marked us with weary eyes and expressionless faces.

However, our hearts which had long been numb, learned to feel again, as soft and honest tears went by. Though we did not know exactly who we were or where we were going, everything was there and before us. It was a time of discovery and rediscovery, a struggle for peace and intimacy. It was a period of re-visitation where I sought and found the child within me—a child whom I had abandoned long ago and to whose most basic yearnings I had become quite deaf. Meeting myself in this way was an immense risk and an intimidating challenge. The most difficult thing for one to do is to take the path which leads to oneself. Each day as I took another small but invaluable step towards myself, the gulf between who I really was and who I appeared to be grew slightly smaller. I learned to accept those things I could not change, and I struggled to change the things I could. I discovered how to feel with spontaneity, rather than artificiality, how to admit my weaknesses, acknowledge my virtues, fulfill my needs, eliminate my more greedy wants, how to forgive without forgetting and love without possessing. I discovered how to love life and myself and how to celebrate both. I had once been a segment without direction or resolve, but behind those good, strong walls, I found the missing peace and became vital and complete and able to stand on my own feet. The ground felt firmer, the sun brighter, the earth warmer.

They grew with me, and we loved each other with a love that was unique as the individual blade and perennial as the grass. The winter snows melted into rain, and the frozen ground became soft and green and ready for cultivating. We watched each other come and go as those before us had done and those after us were sure to do. A year has passed since the time when I first surrendered myself and my inhibitions behind those doors, and yet our separate paths have never crossed again. Still, I see clearly now why we were what we were to one another. We were not children of a lesser God nor even of a different God. We were similarly marked by our individual pasts, and somewhere in our psyche, we had made the choice less chosen and travelled the road less travelled. It has made all the difference.

Isaiah Watas Cox

Isaiah

I grew up in isolation from the world; in the Middle of Nowhere, Idaho USA. Our family lived on the main Salmon River, four miles above the confluence with the South Fork. In the surrounding two million acres there were only about fifteen other human inhabitants.

We lived with my great uncle Sylvan Ambrose Hart, known to readers of *Field and Stream* and *National Geographic*, as Buckskin Bill, Last of the Mountain Men. Sylvan had come to the river with my great-great-grandfather in 1932 and had lived as a hermit for nearly fifty years. Like his Apache and pioneering ancestors, he bored his own rifles, hammered his own copper pots, and used elk furs for blankets.

Since no hospitals existed on Salmon River, my parents came out of the valley to have children. I was born in Calgary, Alberta. I was named Isaiah Watas Cox—the name, like myself, a mix of Biblical, Native American, and English culture.

Since no schools existed on the Salmon River, my parents enrolled us kids in a home study program with Calvert School in Baltimore, Maryland. Calvert was originally set up before the turn of the century to teach Foreign Service and military children abroad. We were sent books and supplies and tested ourselves eight times a year. The tests were sent to Baltimore for grading via the mail plane which landed, once every few weeks, four miles down-river. Calvert taught me a lot; I learned the self-discipline of pacing myself. I learned how to teach myself from books, without constant supervision. But most of all, I learned that learning was not a function of time but of effort. School was not a chore. I found that at many times, I enjoyed it. Except for reading on the sly, studying was the best way to avoid real work—like hauling wood.

We continued Calvert through grade school, even after we

moved to a more accessible mountaintop in Oregon. There was a conflict in my family over the issue of High School. My mother felt it was a necessity—that "real" High School was our last chance of avoiding a life of social barbarism. My father had no difficulty with us becoming social barbarians. It was a family tradition.

My father was born in Wichita, Kansas; the son of a wheat farmer who despised farming. My mother, on the other hand, was born in Detroit, Michigan and lived a "normal" urban life. My father's family has always had a strong streak of pioneering in its blood. We've always built our own houses with our own hands. We've always lived far away from towns. My Uncle Sylvan said that only a poor man has to live where he can see his neighbors. My father's ancestors were pioneers in the "West" when the West was Tennessee, when the West was Kansas, and when the West was Idaho. In the process, the family picked up Apache blood, Swedish blood, and English blood.

The pioneer blood was fired up again when my father's business became involved in mineral exploration in the Canadian North. The Arctic is truly the last frontier on Earth. There is nothing in existence that rivals the feelings of desolation that the emptiness, the solitude, the countless barren cliffs and dead lakes convey to a person standing alone in the cold wind on Melville Peninsula.

But the wilderness alone, despite its attraction for me, has never been enough. We may have been barbarians, but my father always insisted on us being educated barbarians. My parents, while living in Idaho, wrote their Ph.D. dissertations for Columbia. The pioneers in the family were inevitably stand-out intellectuals for their time. My Swedish great-grandmother graduated from college in 1904. My Grandfather attended Harvard in an officer training program for the navy during WWII. Even Buckskin Bill had a B.A. in English from the University of Oklahoma and worked on a Masters in Petroleum Engineering from the same school.

Although we lived in the wilderness and loved it, we have never had any illusions about nature. Nature is not benign. At Catlin I am bombarded by the cliché of the alienation of man, particularly White Western Man from nature. Many of my friends are searching for the "pure wilderness untainted by man's corrupting influence." They believe that Mother Nature is always good and benevolent, while Western Man is always greedy and exploitative. I grew up knowing that nature is not always good and not always benevolent and that when man comes up against nature one on one, for real, not in Thoreau's fashion, nature kills. According to Uncle Sylvan, Henry David Thoreau was a dilettante. After all, he took the train into Boston whenever he wanted a good dinner. There were no trains on Salmon River. On Salmon River nature capriciously killed at least one member of every family in every generation, including mine. *National Geographic* made my Uncle Sylvan into a cult-hero, and in the sixties he served to perpetuate the myth of the Noble Savage. But Uncle Sylvan was not the Noble Savage. He was as a man with a deep love of books and learning.

If the Noble Savage lived anywhere in North America in the 1960s, he lived in the Canadian Arctic. The Inuit I know on Melville Peninsula had lived close to a state of nature before 1968. They lived a life of severe exposure and under the constant threat of starvation. At times they had to kill their own children and they practiced female infanticide. The old men have no illusions about the Noble Savage. The native population in the entire circum-polar region never exceeded 20,000 people until western man came with houses, oil, and food. But houses, oil, and food are not enough. Survival, in and of itself, is not enough. Many Inuit have exchanged a life of cold and starvation for a life of depression, rootlessness, and suicide. Uncle Sylvan used to say that only very stupid or very bright people could survive in the wilderness. Those in between went mad.

My family has lived closer to Nature than anyone else I know south of the Tree Line. I know that the good life is possible, although difficult, without electricity and plumbing. It is not possible without books.

Realization Essays

How do you use your experiences to change and grow? The "realization essay" can show how thoughtful, sensitive, and responsive you are, and writing it may give you even more insight.

One incident rarely changes a person's life. Trying to persuade the reader that, for example, a single football game suddenly revolutionized your personality is likely to sound (and be) contrived rather than profound. Nevertheless, discussing a specific, important experience can be a great way to express a change or an idea that has developed over time.

The first essay, *Why I Love Jesus*, is a frank account of alienation and hypocrisy. Though the tone is sometimes bitter, the cynicism is infectious. The author took a risk, to be sure, but it paid off. An admissions officer at UNC/Chapel Hill uses this essay as an example for applicants.

The second essay struck home to a large number of our early readers. It has excellent insight, but its strongest attribute is the writer's ability to dissolve bitterness with humor and understanding.

An embarrassing, comic event taught Elizabeth McLeer to laugh at herself. Family bankruptcy forced the next applicant to mature quickly and encouraged him to get involved in charity. A visit to a pen pal—who happened to be a prison inmate—gave the next writer his life philosophy.

You sense these writers were already on the way to their "realization" when something happened to crystallize their thinking, to be a catalyst for change. But effectively describing a profound moment—and its lasting effect—is tough, and it takes effort to give credibility and color to the momentous realization.

Melanie Sumner

Why I Love Jesus

Around the age of 13, I was transformed from a little sunshine into something equivalent to Satan's spawn. I do not know why I suddenly began saying, "shut-up", smoking cigarettes, and attending Sunday School alone in the church parking lot. My mother was convinced that it was the hand of Lucifer. Something had to be done.

Our church, a down-home, folksy, Baptist one, was having a Youth Retreat. A Youth Retreat is a weekend spent somewhere in the boonies where youths can have fun and rededicate their lives to God. Fledglings to the house of God and old-timers that have strayed from the path are particularly encouraged to come. I was one of the strays. My mother saddled me with pencils, several variations of the Bible, a helpful little book entitled *Why I Love Jesus*, and, at the last minute, a frisbee. I was then packed off with a dozen other youths to Gatlinburg, Tennessee.

The bus ride to Gatlinburg was not too bad. I pretended that I loved Jesus too and enjoyed spitting spitballs, climbing upon the luggage racks, and screaming, "McDonald's!" with the rest of the youths. My "McDonald's" did not sound like theirs, though. They all pronounced the "a" with a drawn out twang. Eventually, as it usually does with this age group, the conversation turned to school. The twang got louder, and I heard someone say "ain't". "Where ya going to school?" I was awakened from my intense study of a nearby girl's Docksiders. The stitching was different; they were not real Docksiders at all. I decided that the shoes were a forgery, an economy brand from K-Mart. I had delayed in answering the casual question, and now all eyes were upon me.

"Uh, Darlington," I mumbled. There was a slight silence. It was an ugly word. Darlington meant money, preppy clothes, and smart people: Heathens mostly. Since I was a snob from

98

Darlington, most of the young disciples didn't speak to me for the rest of the weekend.

The lodge for our Youth Retreat was situated on top of a grassy hillside, complete with mountainous views and clean, swirling streams that ended in tranquil blue pools. I was impressed. If there were a God, I certainly might find Him in these celestial surroundings. The church leaders had other things in mind. As always, there was a smattering of wholesome religious fun. Fun was mandatory. Several times during the day we were all compelled to gather around a tarnished, tuneless piano and sing to Jesus. Young faces glowing with the love of Christ turned to glare at me because I was not singing. I personally thought Jesus would have better taste in music.

We also played a softball game. This game was organized with hidden Christian motives by Lennie The Youth Director. Lennie was a short, pink, pudgy Christian who giggled, "O.K. gang, are we ready for Bible softball?"

"Ain't never heard of it," replied a wayward youngster. Evidently Lennie saw humor in this because he had a mild fit of giggling. Then with unrestrained joy at having invented such a novel game, he exclaimed, "You guys are gonna be Philistines and Israelites!" He emitted another silly giggle. I began to doubt the authenticity of his gender. Is God like that? What if God is a nerd? We played Bible softball, and I was exiled the second inning for uttering pagan words after my third strike. I was marched back to the lodge by a Youth Director Assistant and ordered to repent and wait for Lennie.

I decided to repent while exploring the surrounding forest of our camp. It was calm in the woods, and I enjoyed wandering around and climbing upon the huge rock formations scattered about. I settled myself on a particularly comfortable rock and decided to try and find God. I considered my numerous sins and transgressions, and failing to find any way to redeem myself, I began searching through my pockets for a Winston Light. A few puffs of a cigarette always seemed to clear my mind.

Lennie was not his smiling self when I found my way back to our group of cabins. Everyone had gone to the streets of Gatlinburg to convert bad people by singing to them and giving away free "God Loves You" mugs. Lennie thought we should have a little talk or "rap" as he put it. I thought not and so tried to speed things up by congenially admitting to being the

Antichrist. Lennie The Youth Director was not amused. I endeavored to make him feel more comfortable by giggling. I do not think he liked me much after that.

The last night of every Youth Retreat is the biggest. It is an evening of burning confession and mass conversion. The night was hot and coal black as we all seated ourselves around the huge bonfire. Lennie gave an inspiring sermon warning us that time is short. The amber red of the roaring flames reflected on the circle of little Christian faces. It reminded me of hell. At last the preaching drew to a close and the finale was upon us.

"If you feel that Gawd has touched your heart, come; come and promise your soul to Him. He is calling one and all. Yes, He is calling you!" There was some nervous whispering and murmurs of "Reckon we gotta . . ." The first little lamb edged her way forward and the rest followed noisily, like a herd of dirty, stupid sheep. They all went. They were all called, all touched by the mysterious hand of the Lord. Each renewed believer walked to the center of the ever narrowing circle to shake Lennie's hand and sit closer to the fire—closer so that if you squinted your eyes it looked like they were in the fire, holding Lennie's hand, smiling. The fire burned lower until there was only a flicker among the charred embers. And still one black soul sat away from the saved ones, one black one still believed.

Name Withheld

Ever watch "My Three Sons" on T.V.? I'm not an avid
television viewer, but whenever I'd watch it when I was little it
always struck me as rather odd. "Pop" always smiled
benevolently and gave wise counsel over dinner, while meals
with my own "Pop" always consisted of an awkward silence
occasionally punctuated by a sarcastic remark from my father in
some impersonal restaurant. Just recently, however, my father
and I met for dinner after a long and regrettable estrangement;
what happened that night played more like a scene from "My
Three Sons" than anything of my previous experience, and my
reactions to it made me understand both my father and myself
with greater insight and maturity than ever before.

Perhaps all children see their parents as demi-gods capable of
incredible feats but incapable of fault or weakness. I'd always
seen my father that way, but was awakened from this somewhat
euphoric state early in my childhood when my parents' divorce
and my father's apparent neglect shattered my ideal of fatherly
perfection. Not only did my father not measure up to Fred
MacMurray, but he seemed to have nothing but faults. My
attitude spilled over into other areas of my young life; just as
Plato had conceived of a perfect example of everything in his
Theory of Forms, a little Jesse had already established in his
mind certain idealistic standards for all people and things in his
life. I must admit, these standards of perfection made me a
somewhat compulsive little boy who was often left disillusioned.

The differences between my father and myself were further
aggravated by a conflict of interests: Dad would visit on
weekends, dragging me away from a good book for a game of
baseball where my ineptitude left me feeling deeply
embarrassed. In a way, though, I believe what I saw as my
father's un-intellectuality made me strive all the more in the
opposite direction. "Chip" may have had a sweet and doting
father, but I'm willing to bet my socks that "Chip" can't read
ancient Greek!

Thus, I found myself a bit surprised and confused when my father and I finally began to communicate. He told me that, although we didn't have common interests, he held a greater regard for mine, that he admired and was almost jealous of my strength of will in resisting his influence and in pursuing what I loved. He apologized for his inability to communicate and for the neglect that had prevented a close relationship between us, and he told me that he'd always been proud of me, of my achievements and performances and of the person I had become.

As he spoke, I realized that the very fact that we were speaking meant that, I, too, had long since purged the choler of my disillusioned resentment that had maintained the wall between us. This reconciliation left me feeling good, not only about my father but about myself. I understood how I had changed from a cynical little tot into an optimistic young man. I realize now that hoping for perfection, that creating idols, is a frustrating and fruitless pursuit; I am even grateful for imperfections in the people and things that I love because those imperfections allow me to more fully understand what love is, and because I sense that my own imperfections, too, are forgivable. This fall, I was outraged by a change my school had implemented in the direction of a more standardized curriculum, a change decidedly for the worse. I channeled my energy into a constructive campaign to rally student support and to offer alternate solutions. I was able to do this because I had come to realize that an institution may be flawed but still amenable to change, and that it is everyone's responsibility to work to perfect it rather than wallow in disillusioned resignation.

Perhaps my early experience of having my ideals shattered helped me to develop a realistic outlook. After a period of disillusionment, I believe I matured into a heightened awareness of myself and others. Compassion and self-awareness are qualities I prize most and ones that in some measure I now possess.

Whereas I was once an exacting perfectionist, I have grown into a person with an almost pathological need to understand and help other people. It is almost as if I am making up for lost time which I spent expecting too much from others; my adolescent life has been spent in efforts, both on a personal level and in schoolwide activities, to make others feel comfortable with themselves and proud of their own achievements. I believe very strongly in modesty and social courtesy; at the very least boasting makes others uncomfortable. My tendency to strive for excellence, however, has not disappeared, but evolved: now I see being "perfect" as being tolerant and compassionate, towards others and towards myself.

I believe that all children defy their parents and that part of growing up involves the gradual acceptance of faults. It may be that my parents' divorce interrupted this natural flow in my own life, but it also hastened it. I am better off having grown up with obstacles, and my reconciliation with my father has provided a vantage point from which I can look back and understand that I have finally achieved a balance between acceptance and perfectionism. Looking back now, I can't believe that I ever compared such a decent and complex man as my father to some two-dimensional character on a T.V. program that never got particularly good ratings anyway. And, when you get right down to it, how great could a man be if he names his son "Chip?"

Elizabeth McLeer

One of my earliest forays into the boy-girl social whirl ended in comical humiliation for me. At the age of fourteen, I spied an attractive local teenage boy; I enquired about his eligibility from a friend, and learned that he was a young gentleman who strictly "preferred blondes," which I emphatically was not. Having previously borrowed an older friend's high-style blonde wig and achieved what my juvenile mentality then deemed as positive masculine feedback, I arranged an introduction with this boy while wearing said hairpiece. He appeared enthusiastic about me, so we set up our first "group" date for Christmas Eve.

The evening started well; midnight mass was lovely; afterwards, walking to someone's house for a small festivity, the scene was idyllic: snow falling, boys and girls walking along, singing, laughing, me strolling proudly with my new beau in all my shimmering, well-coiffured blondness. Suddenly, ahead, a narrow pathway blocked mainly by a large tree with low-hanging branches forced us to walk single-file; as I bent my head I felt a branch forcefully graze it, but thought nothing of it. A few seconds later, however, my girlfriend, walking behind me, suddenly shouted out, "Betsy, look!" I turned to see her outstretched hand pointing to the offending branch from which I now observed a pale, strange-looking, long-haired animal with no face swaying in the breeze. Simultaneously, I felt a sudden chill hit my head. Egads! The jig was up. That fair, furry critter was no animal, it was my wig. I was revealed to all as the "blah" brownette phony that I really was! While my escort stared incredulously back and forth between the wig and my head and rebuked me with a harsh, "I thought you were a real blond," I made haste to grab the wig and return it to my head, as if to turn back time and erase this spectacle from everyone's mind. Alas, I was one step too slow for one of the other boys, who whipped it off the tree, plopped it on his head and started prancing around while squealing mincingly, "Look at me. I'm a blonde." He then made a forward pass with the wig to another boy, and another, and another, each of whom took his turn at this demeaning form of female impersonation, while I ran desperately from one boy to the next, vainly trying to recapture my wig and all the observers to this scene bent doubled over in hysterical laughter. Finally, realizing the futility of my chase and the absurdity of my posture, I bowed to the inevitable and joined in the laughter. I spent the rest of the evening at the party reliving my shame as the boys re-told and re-enacted this episode for all who had not witnessed it.

Unfortunately, my date was true to his principles: he paid no further serious attention to me, that night or ever. I learned from that occasion that, unfortunately, some males did have very high, narrowly-defined standards of physical female beauty. On the other hand, I also learned that not all males are so rigid. Shortly after that evening, I developed very happy long-term social relationships with not one, but two, boys present that evening who informed me that they noticed and became interested in me because I was "fun to tease, could take a joke" and appeared vulnerable and, therefore, approachable. Indeed, several of the other girls present later confessed to me that they, too, liked me better after that escapade. Thus, I discovered the very fundamental and useful psychological principle that most people do prefer others who are not always in perfect control, but who are all too humanly flawed. Finally, with time, I realized that what my mother had always told me was true: that in the long-run, the events in youth which seemed so shatteringly humiliating, were those which, in maturity, one laughed about the most, especially when oneself was the object of the fun.

Name Withheld

I have been told that when I was born my parents' friends lovingly nicknamed me, "The Little Prince." This was because my father had let everyone know that if the baby turned out to be a boy, he would be the first son, of a first son, of a first son, of a first son. This is very auspicious lineage in my father's country and in the Sikh culture in particular. Everyone predicted a comfortable and carefree life.

Growing up in New York I saw examples of homelessness and hunger almost every day, yet in my early years those problems never touched me on a personal level. My only experience in community service was helping to fill Easter baskets for children at Bellevue and shopping for an anonymous Christmas gift every year for an unknown baby at the hospital. The realm of poverty seemed like a completely different world; a world that would never affect me, and a world I could certainly never alter.

About midway through Seventh Grade, my attitude began to undergo a profound change. After several years of business problems, my father declared bankruptcy. At the time, I never fully understood what was going on, but I did know my life was being turned upside down. Shortly after the school year ended, we lost our home, the place I had lived for my entire life, and moved to my grandfather's house in New Jersey. For the first four months of the next school year, I commuted to Manhattan every day for school and every Sunday for church. I left the house at 5:45 AM and got home at 6:30 PM. My grades and social life suffered, but there was nothing I could do to change my living situation.

I remember one night I wanted to go to a concert with some of my friends. My mother told me I could go, but that we would have to sleep in the church overnight because it would be unsafe to catch a bus to New Jersey at such a late hour. That's when it really hit me. For months I had been living through an uncomfortable situation, but did not fully understand what it meant. That night, when my mother told me I had to sleep in a church in order to go out with my friends, I realized I was homeless.

We moved seven more times during eighth and ninth grades, and I often did not know where I would be living in the coming month. We lived in a series of short-term sublets or apartment sat for friends who were away. My life was being dominated by forces I could neither control nor understand. Since tenth grade we have been able to stay in the same place, and we are all very happy to be putting our lives back together.

Uncomfortable as our temporary arrangements had been, I realized even then that there are many people in this world who have suffered much more than we had. We never had to face the prospect of actually living on the streets, and we always had plenty to eat, but I came to understand a little of how it might feel to be in the shoes of a homeless person. I feel that this experience has done more to shape my character and personality than any other event in my life. I emerged a more mature, more aware, and more sensitive human being. I have become very involved in my community, and people are more involved with me. I like to think that this development would have happened anyway, but perhaps not on such a deeply personal level.

Most importantly, the problems of the world no longer seem distant to me, and I have developed a sense of responsibility to help find some of their solutions. I have worked extensively as a volunteer in my church's dinner program for the homeless and helped to start a new humanitarian club in my school. Every homeless person I have talked to has a story about how he or she got on the streets, and I have learned that most of their situations started off not much differently from mine. My story has a happy ending, but too many others do not. I now understand that not only can I make a difference in the lives of these people, but I also have a responsibility to do so. Looking back over the past five years, my life seems almost like a tale in ancient mythology. I imagine myself as the young, immature hero who must experience a period of trials as part of his quest for eventual maturity.

Name Withheld

I only met him once. I guess you could say "met." The thick glass partition between us was relatively clean—not too scratched—and although the phones were old and the crackling lines hid subtle nuances in our voices, I could understand his words.

"It's like hell in here, isn't it," he said—and then caught himself—I was only eleven.

"Yes!" I wanted to scream, "It *is* hell!" but I didn't. I smiled a vague smile that could mean whatever he wanted it to.

"I'm glad you came," he said, "I don't get many visitors."

It was the Saturday before we moved to North Carolina. I had awakened that morning early. My mother and I had driven the sixty miles to Trenton—me bouncing excitedly in my seat, talking and sometimes singing—reading his letters over and over . . .

The building appeared. It was stone and iron, cement and barbed wire, hard and cold. I remember wondering how he must have felt—approaching that gate—knowing he would not leave for a long, long time. We entered.

"Hi, Marshall, I'm Ray," he said. Although his face and voice were those of a stranger, I recognized his words. We talked.

I cried as we drove away. Some people told my mother it was irresponsible to take me to a prison when I was so young—I had nightmares about it afterwards. Now I think I understand why she took me. Ray and I had been close pen-pals for three years, and he was my friend. My mother knew that friends are worth late night distress phone calls and long, teary walks and forgiveness when you're angry. And friends are worth a few nightmares.

"I have been feeling a little lonely lately," Ray wrote my mother, "(the inside of this prison can be very depressing at times) but with your and Marshall's visit today, you may never know how happy you made me feel."

People ask me what it was like to write to a criminal, and I

108

must admit that often there was a tugging between the idea that "this is Ray, your buddy and confidant," and that "he did *something* to get in there." From this conflict rose one of the few truths I have found to be absolute—all people have good in them. If a "hardened" criminal—categorized as the epitome of evil—can show tenderness and sincerity, who cannot? At some time in his life, the good in Ray was brushed aside while the criminal blossomed; and some other time, a little later, someone touched him. Someone showed him love and understanding, and the Ray I knew was born. I learned from Ray that to enjoy life, I must search out good—in others and in myself—and nurture and develop that.

One day the letters stopped coming. Everything I sent was returned: "nonexistent address." I never found out what happened to him.

For years I almost expected him to walk up to me on the street, and in a way he did. Like Jesus—who is every hungry, naked, sick man—Ray became every lonely, every angry, every misunderstood person with a seed of good in him. Every stranger. Everyone.

Thought Essays

The serious, philosophical "thought essay" is perhaps the most difficult essay to write. The best examples demonstrate an intellectually curious and disciplined mind, but even the best can be hard to read. Frequently, the essay loses its impact because students digress from the original point and allow their logic to become muddled by "ten-dollar words" and complicated strings of sentences.

Most students get too abstract when they discuss philosophical concepts. When you write about an abstract idea, link it to a tangible example with which the reader can identify. For example, you might use the death of your dog as a starting point for a discussion of religious philosophy. Remember, too, that admissions officers are pressed for time. They don't have all day to wade through your prose and mull over your deep, brilliant insights.

Interestingly, when we asked classmates to submit essays to us, more than one-third were "thought essays," and almost all were tough to read. But when admissions officers sent us their favorites, only a few were on philosophical topics. After all, if you had to read three hundred essays a day, would you rather read Immanuel Kant or Mark Twain?

We don't want to scare you, though. A "thought essay" might be perfect for you. The essays in this section are both interesting and effective.

Alicia Jordan's, Joaquin Feliciano's, and Jamie Mayer's essays are notable for their use of an armadillo, an imaginary friend, and an inchworm respectively to introduce their deep ponderings. Mayer's inchworm essay—one of our favorites—is so effective because it indicates, in the words of his admissions officer, "the ability to leave one's own perspective behind to see the world from the perspective of another age, culture, sex, or background. It shows unusual insight and perception, and the writing is simply superb."

Ross Howard Reynolds

"Armadillos are stupid creatures . . ."

The advice of my friend, Danny Maginty—"We used to hit
them with sticks in my backyard in Texas. They would roll into
a ball and let us play soccer with them all over the place. They
are the stupidest creatures I have ever known."
Our usual Spanish class was in session in nearly every usual
way, except one. Today we conversed in English. It was a rare
occurrence: Dr. Keck would not permit it to happen again until
a month later, when the seniors of the class would be leaving it
forever. It would be one of two times English was permitted that
year. For now the seniors about me were pleased not to have to
stumble over the obstacles of "another" language, and I sat back
listening, taking a break from what had been a tense day.
Will Owen was talking, "We used to hunt them at night on an
island in the middle of the Mississippi. The first thing they did
when we shot them was run, jump in the water. They can't
swim."
We laughed nervously, but soon the jokes took us over. Seven
of our friends, seniors and juniors, had been expelled for the use
of illegal drugs. They were packing their bags that day, leaving
us quietly to figure out that part of them we had hardly known.
Dr. Keck knew that most of us were too shocked to learn
anything about Spanish that day. He had not even thought of
holding class, but he expected the day to be a learning
experience. He declared an open discussion; so instead of
approaching the subject directly, we all sat about discussing
something else.
David Haddock was the only one who had never seen a live
armadillo in his life. He had, however, seen many a crushed one
strewn across the highways.
I myself had a chance to observe the creatures earlier that
year, on Cumberland Island, Georgia. They were very
nearsighted animals, and one allowed me to approach him very

closely. He was small, similar to a rat with a hairy shell over him. When frightened the armadillo always returned to a certain palmetto bush for safety.

Armadillos are one of the few creatures which have remained unchanged since prehistoric times. Since its origin the armadillo has always been a traveler. If the environment changed, it would move. It continued moving until it ended up in protected reserves like Cumberland, and South Georgia—where some say the biggest change in the last fifty years was the TV satellite.

The final conclusion of our discussion was that if you ever had a hand in the making of your second life, don't be an armadillo.

It's a piece of advice I take very seriously in my present life. It goes beyond the armadillo's complete refusal to adapt. It is the stubbornness with which it clings to its actions, excludes the real situation, and the awkwardness in which it exists.

It seems that we are often trying to flee problems that originate in the part of us that wants to be an armadillo. Yet we always flee back to our palmetto bushes. It is our instinct to cling to a mode of thinking, an experience, a lesson, or a simple substance that has given us success with coping and existing in the past.

Our only boast may be that we can cling to more complicated thoughts and actions, for we often see ourselves throwing up our hairy armor against unrestricted thought. In truth we may never escape the plight of the armadillo.

Yet it is the progress of this direction to which I have dedicated myself, and which I envision as an education. Whether there is an ideal intelligence which clings to nothing, or just a vague clinging to the most complicated thoughts the human brain can endure, it is my hope to work continually forward and escape the problems of becoming an armadillo.

Joaquin Feliciano

The one person who has most influenced my life is Rachel Hooke. Rachel is seventeen years old, has long red hair and blue eyes, and enjoys cycling and cross country running. What sets her apart from others is that she exists only in my mind and on the pages of a creative journal that I have been keeping for the past four years.

Since my first journal entry, Rachel has evolved from a handy character name in short stories to a deeply developed "person" in her own right. I am continually fascinated by the strength of the bond I feel between us, even though she does not exist in any physical way. In my journal I have supplied her with a nuclear family, a high school to attend, and even a pet St. Bernard named Lewis. More than just a deeply thought-out player in an elaborate make-believe world, she has become real to the point where I have found myself comparing her to actual people.

While looking over some of my old journal entries recently, I realized that who she is and that the changes she has gone through up to this point say a great deal about who I was and who I am now. She can be used as a lens to bring me, her creator, into focus.

Rachel's first consistent description was of a shy, quiet and unhappy girl who had few friends and spent much time alone. It was easy to envisage myself meeting her, falling in love and then taking her away to an isolated island to live happily ever after. Rachel was a very simple, flat character who, while having a very distinct personality, was still lacking in human complexity and range of emotion. This naive, black and white portrayal of her reflects who I was at the time. I myself was shy and introverted, having dreams of meeting someone and then forgetting the rest of the world in favor of this one, perfect mate. When I entered the Ninth grade among both new students and classmates I had known since kindergarten, I noticed an inability on my part to feel comfortable around them. I originally attributed this problem to a lack of maturity on their part, but now I see that the root of the problem lay with me. I was very distressed at feeling alienated and distant from my peers, and rather than try to remedy the situation, I withdrew farther into myself.

Over a period of about six months, Rachel slowly changed into an aggressive, fiercely independent person very much in control of who she was and who she wanted to be. She was competitive and confident in herself and her abilities. This personality was further enhanced by her physical description: she was a tall, athletic, and fiery-haired young woman given to loudly and sometimes violently expressing her ideas and opinions. While at first glance this seems to show a dramatic change in my character, I think that Rachel's new persona serves as a magnification of the situation shown in her original image.

While this change was taking place in my journal, two important happenings were taking place in the real world. At a summer music camp I regularly attended, I became involved in a serious relationship with a girl who had many Rachel-like qualities. During those short weeks, I was able to forget all the loneliness of my life at home and, as I had envisioned happening with Rachel, my whole world centered around this one person. Of course, at the end of the summer, I had to return home to Maryland and she to California. I was emotionally crushed, the first few weeks away from her were the most miserable moments of my life. To add to this, my parents became interested in a new religion and were pressuring me into it as well. In their zealousness to promote this new ideology, I felt that I was losing contact with my family. I felt truly alone. I spent long hours writing about Rachel in order to escape the loneliness that surrounded me. I was intent upon standing alone, without relying on friends or family to support me. By making Rachel so independent and strong-willed, I had created a role-model, projecting a goal that I was trying to reach. I was withdrawing further and further from the people around me, resisting my own strong urges to find friends and to feel accepted by a group of people in an attempt to obtain the level of independence where I had placed Rachel.

Rachel is currently an athletic and attractive girl who, while still shy, is less withdrawn and more interested in the people around her. Like her previous personality, she is still very independent, but realizes the importance of respecting and communicating with others. She is much more complex than before, much more human than her previous selves. I like to think that my ability to make her current identity more real comes from my own personal maturation. I have started to come to terms with my conflicting desires to be independent from others, yet accepted by them at the same time. Like Rachel, I try to follow my own feelings and opinions, but am always open to what others have to say.

Somewhere in my personal world of self-pity, I realized that what I really needed, and indeed desired, were friends that I could talk to and feel supported by. As a Junior, I made many new friends and while my family situation grew no better, I was able to face these problems in a new light because I no longer had to face them alone. Rather than a savior who will take me away from the world I now live in, I see Rachel as a companion, someone to share my experiences with. When I read my most recent writing, I am happy to see a more complex, round, human element in Rachel that was not there only a few short months ago.

Since my first journal entry on 5 August, 1985 at 10:24 PM, I have gone through many shifts and changes in myself and how I relate to the people around me. Rachel Hooke, a prominent figure in all of my writing, has been there with me, going through some of the same changes and conflicts. Looking back, I am glad that I kept a personal record of my progress in the form of my creative journal. I can only speculate about who Rachel will be after I graduate from high school and move into new areas and meet new people.

Jamie Mayer

I showed myself an inchworm this morning and now I feel guilty. Walking up the road beneath the leafy ceiling, I stopped myself short, face-to-face with a solitary green strand. The strand squirmed slowly, waiting for me to look closer. It was an inchworm, but it was not inching. It was spiraling on a central axis, like a single, floating strip of DNA. I never would have seen this swiveling little guy had his plump, new body and its delicate thread which was attached to an overhead branch not been hanging directly in my path.

Our eyes work on a now-you-see-it, now-you-don't system. One either focuses on the very near, or, as too many people do, on the distant horizon, blindly pointed off in one direction or another. Because of our human-proportioned lifestyle, things on an inchworm's measuring scale lose their impact. It is a "man-sized" world—bigger and better, new and improved. An inch just doesn't get you very far in our age of jet planes, space travel, and olympic long jump records of over 29 feet. Man has developed a knack for using himself as a ruler against which all else is measured. How egotistical we are.

So this morning, after nodding goodbye to my small green acquaintance, who was still swirling about like a circus performer with a rope between his teeth, I continued up the road, determined to look outside the proportions of the world I had grown up with. It was difficult. My eyes fought for their right to look through, rather than on the air; to a careful observer it might have looked as if I had a severe focusing disorder.

I am guilty. Guilty of belonging to this self-centered group that imposes its measurements and physical limitations on the rest of the natural world. It's true that the plants and animals which we can and cannot see don't realize the structure we have dropped them into. I am glad of this. Even the dolphin, said to be one of the most "intelligent" creatures after man, can swim the ocean, oblivious to the cities, borders and rules men have set up for themselves. I envy the dolphin, slippery flippers paddling, silly without-a-care jaws grinning. Intelligence without useless complication.

There is a Dr. Seuss story about a goofy elephant named Horton who discovered a tiny universe existing on a particle of drifting dust. Only one of the dust creatures believes there is anything beyond the tiny sphere, but in order to save the "planet" from destruction, its inhabitants must be convinced of life beyond their own world. Similarly, our only hope is to learn to acknowledge the worlds which exist around us. The worm was not aware of me or the human-oriented world I live in, but because I am able to, I feel an important responsibility to respect and protect these parallel universes.

Essays About Activities

More than any other topic, college applicants write about their activities. This makes sense, especially if an activity takes up a lot of your time, but be careful not to just repeat what you've already written in other sections of your application.

The key to a good "activities essay" (or to any essay, for that matter) is to *personalize* and *analyze*. Why do you like to windsurf? What does basketball mean to you, and how does describing your jump shot give the reader insight to your personality? As president of the Chess Club, what have you learned and what have you observed—and what does that mean?

In the first essay, Joe Clifford explains what sports have *really* taught him, not what sports are supposed to teach him. Joe challenges the usual sports clichés, and such an essay always shows that you've been thinking.

The "activities essay" can embrace both the mundane and the bizarre. In the next essays, three students create memorable pieces out of seemingly boring topics—cooking, babysitting, and working in a doughnut shop. But each essay reveals its author's personality as well as anything could. If you feel your life is just too conventional to write about, pay close attention to what Barbara Bluestone, Jillian Myrom, and Daniel Ross did. Imagine turning a simple recipe for cranberry bread into an effective presentation of your life and accomplishments! With a little creativity and a lot of hard thought, no topic is too ordinary for a great essay.

Joe Clifford

I am not sure how meaningful this is, but, if I were given the option of being either a well-reknowned intellectual giant or a Cy Young Award-winning baseball player, I would instinctively choose the latter. Sports, especially baseball and basketball, have played a very important role in what college application forms would call "my development as a human being."

When my father was teaching me how to play baseball, he would have me get into a batting stance with my whiffle bat. Then he would purposely throw the whiffle ball directly at the bat so that I could not help but get a hit. Of course, Dad would act exasperated, putting on his "How is a five-year old kid hitting like Babe Ruth against me?" routine. The point is, not suspecting that anything was amiss, I was in my glory. Here I was, five years old, and I was laying waste to anything my six foot, 200 pound father had to offer. Even my young mind appreciated the distinct Oedipal irony. This was heaven.

As I grew older (and began to understand why I was not hitting as perfectly as I had that first day) I continued to crave the black-and-white conflicts of sports. To this day, I still play the same David and Goliath mind-games that I first played with Dad hurling the old whiffle ball at me. For example, if I'm dribbling the ball towards the hoop in a basketball game, I'm saying to myself, "Here's little Joey Clifford taking it in to that intimidating behemoth from Midtown. Oh Goodness! Did you see that? Clifford just destroyed the goon with that sensational move! What a performer!" These mind-games are even more common when I'm pitching in a baseball game. For instance, I'll picture tomorrow's newspaper write-up in my head as I pitch. "Little Joey Clifford was just sensational out there," gushed Coach Jones, "after the fourth time he struck out last year's MVP I just said, 'Holy Smokes, what a performer!' "

I have written about these David and Goliath mind-games I play because they in particular emphasize why sports have been so important in my life. The way I approach sports has been a major influence on the way I approach life.

First of all, I am not the type to say that being a point guard has taught me discipline or that being a pitcher has taught me self-control and balance. I consider sports to be too pure and clean for that kind of specific and corny dissection. But, more generally, I cannot deny that sports have been the crucial factor in how I view life and how I accept challenges of life.

Sports have been called a "microcosm of life." I totally disagree. Baseball games are played in black-and-white in my mind. Life is one big gray area. Sports are simple and direct. Life is not. By way of contrast, sports have shown me that I cannot view life as a "me against the world" proposition as I would on the pitching mound. It is too selfish and egotistical a view for the "real world."

However, there is one area in my life where the David vs. Goliath motif that I learned through sports can be positively applied—how I accept challenges. As the weeks tick by in my senior year, the new challenges multiply at an alarming rate. And I like to accept each of these challenges as though I were the underdog, the "David" so to speak. (I picture a movie poster. "They said it could not be done. But he surprised every one of them.") However, it is in the solving of challenges that these self-serving mind-games have to be thrown out. Dad is not throwing the ball at my whiffle bat anymore. I can accept a challenge as if it were a baseball game. But I cannot solve it by striking someone out. This is what sports have taught me.

Barbara Bluestone

Cranberry Bread

4 c. flour	1 small can frozen orange juice
2 c. sugar	4 T melted butter
3 t. baking powder	2 eggs
1 t. salt	1 c. chopped nuts
1 t. soda	1 pkg. cranberries

I'm not sure that cooking best reflects my personality; I am certainly not the domestic type, but I do enjoy cooking and baking if only because it gives me a chance to meditate and do something constructive at the same time. I think that my personality is what I think of when I have free time to ramble. Not only is the following an overview of my personality but also a delicious recipe.

First the flour and sugar need to be sifted together into a large bowl. Flour reminds me of the powder snow that falls in the West. I was born and raised in Pennsylvania where our snow falls more like sugar, granular and icy, and makes us hardy skiers unlike those spoiled by Western snow. Cold weather also is conducive to reading, which I love to do. I received my first Bobbsey twin book on my sixth birthday and have read my way through birthdays ever since. I just read *A Room With a View* by E. M. Forster and adored it. The baking powder, salt, and soda go in next. I have ceased to measure these any more. My mother taught me that to estimate is easier and sometimes the recipe will turn out better for an innocent mistake and a little adventuring. Always adding more chocolate is one of her ideas of an innocent mistake.

The orange juice needs to be thawed, opened, and added. Orange juice makes me think of poetry. The color is vibrant and the taste is sour, sweet, and tangy all at the same time, just like poetry. I write it and read it in search of new ideas and emotions—writers like John Keats, Emily Dickinson, T.S. Eliot, and Wallace Stevens never let me down. My own poetry allows me a freedom that is not there in prose, ideas that conflict or are confused can just add to the richness of the poetry. The butter needs to be melted, probably a microwave would be easiest. Technology, money and the free market system has done some wonderful things, not just for the art of cooking obviously. When I was younger, I liked to sit on my daddy's lap while he read the newspaper and he would explain to me what the stock market was, the meaning of options, the Dow Jones, etc. I still enjoy watching the stock market and I hope to do a mentorship with a stock analyst this year. All this would account for my goals of majoring in economics and then to work for my M.B.A.

The two eggs should be added to the bowl next. Then the nuts need to be chopped and put in the bowl. My little brother dislikes nuts immensely. He feels that I have betrayed him because I like nuts now, when before we were united against mom for putting nuts in chocolate chip cookies. Jonathan (my brother) calls the school I go to the 'Geek School'. He is wrong. My school is a mix of people that might not know where they are going but they know that they are going somewhere. If I didn't attend the North Carolina School of Science and Mathematics, I know that I would be jealous of those who did. The atmosphere of purpose that exists here is one I hope to also find in college.

The last ingredient is cranberries which need to be chopped in half before being added. Cranberries are autumn which is my favorite season. Fall is cool and shrewd and alive with those who can survive winter.

Grease and flour pans before putting mixture in. Bake at 350° for 50 minutes. Eat well.

Jillian B. Myrom

It seemed I was there every hour of every day of every week when I was in the thick of it. But not for much longer! Today, August 8, 1985, was the last day I was babysitting for the Bowdens. And thank goodness! No more getting up at 7 a.m. on a summer morning, no more peanut butter and jelly every day at noon. I was through with all that. Moving on and moving up to better things. I had a job at Roy Rogers all lined up for me to start the following Monday. Finally, a real job.

I sat down hard in the metal chair in the Bowdens' kitchen and glanced up at the clock. Four thirty-seven, only 53 minutes until Mom and Dad would pull up, hand me a check, and send me home for the last time. Grasping a blue crayon, I leaned over to draw a flower for Anya on her large white paper. Anya was six years old, and handicapped with spina bifida. This caused her spine to curve, which affected her internal organs so much that she was incapable of going to the bathroom. She needed to be catheterized about four times a day in order to relieve her bladder and reduce the possibility of infection or virus. She looked to be closer to the age of three if judged by her size. Her eyes were almond shaped and her features chubby, giving a mongoloid appearance. But I always thought she was beautiful.

Aaron, her older brother by two years, came running into the kitchen, closely followed by his little brother B.J., who was Anya's age.

"Jill? Where are my drawings of Voltron? I want to finish them before Daddy comes home. He promised to photocopy them if I do them in time!" Aaron searched frantically through the shelves next to the sink.

"I don't think they'll be in here, Aaron. Let's check in the den." Aaron and his sidekick scrambled into the next room while I turned back to Anya.

"And as for you!" I beamed down at her eager little smile. I pulled her to my hip, leg braces dangling, and we waltzed into the den when B.J. shouted, "I found 'em, Aaron! I found 'em!

Daddy'll be so proud 'cause we didn't lose them!" Relief flooded the youthful face of Aaron, replacing his worried expression of a moment before.

"What are all the pictures for?" I asked.

"We're gonna send them to Channel 29 for their Voltron drawing contest."

"Yeah! And if we win, our pictures'll be on T.V.!" B.J. added, handing them to me.

"Well, if it were up to me, I sure would put them on T.V.! These are great, you guys!" And they were. I never knew a six and eight year old could be so artistic.

"Let's play a game, Jill! I wanna play 'Life'!" Anya sounded so excited that I figured I could play her favorite game just one more time.

"Do you guys want to play?" I asked, carefully setting Anya down against the sofa, mindful of her feeble legs. I saw the VCR clock silently turn to 4:45 out of the corner of my eye.

"Oops! You know what? It's quarter of five, and you know what that means!" I said, pulling Anya up to me again. "Time to cath you!"

I carried her up to her room and laid her down so that I could catheterize her. Anya was always so good about it, as she was about all of her health problems, such as the operations she'd had and the therapy that she required once a week.

Clutching her Cabbage Patch doll, she said, "You cath me and I'll cath Gilbert, O.K.?," turning her deep blue eyes to me for approval.

"Sounds like a good idea to me," I replied, musing that perhaps Anya wasn't such a burden after all.

We returned to the den to find the game already set up.

"We're all gonna play, O.K. Jill?"

"That's great—the more, the better!" I resat Anya by the sofa and help B.J. count out the money.

"Jill? Can we go to the park tomorrow and eat lunch there like we did the last time? That was fun."

"You know what, you guys? I can't take you anywhere anymore because today is my last day here with you. Your mom and dad are going to take some days off to be with you guys." They all sat quietly for a moment (which, upon looking back, was quite rare).

"You mean you're not coming back? Why? Don't you like us anymore?" Aaron's pout troubled me more than his words.

"Of course I like you! It's just that your mom and dad won't need me anymore this summer, that's all."

"Oh." B.J.'s eyes were downcast as he absently fumbled with the cards.

"Come on, you guys! Don't look so sad! I'm still your friend. You can come see me working at Roy's! Maybe I'll sneak you some extra fries if you don't misbehave. Would you like that?" I leaned over and tickled a giggle out of Aaron.

"And you!" I said to Anya. "We've got to get you a pair of those funky chicken sunglasses! What do you say to that?" I pushed her hair behind her ear and got a big smile in return.

Then out of the blue we heard a car door slam and two pairs of footsteps on the back steps.

"They're home! Mommy and Daddy are home!" The two boys ran out to greet them while I pulled Anya to my hip for perhaps the last time.

"Hi Jill! How've they been? Not giving you too much trouble, I hope," Mrs. Bowden smiled, placing her thin briefcase on the kitchen floor with a smart click of metal on tile.

"No, they've been great." I attempted a smile as I placed Anya down in her specially-made chair.

Her husband filled out a check while I stood looking at the three children who felt like my own. They waited in the kitchen while I retrieved my sneakers from the den. I tied my shoelaces tightly while they thanked me for the help I'd given them that summer. I told them that it had been my pleasure, and realized subconsciously that I was speaking the truth.

B.J. then looked up from under his Phillies' cap and said, "We'll miss you, Jill."

Unable to speak, I hugged each of them before I left their house for the very last time. Moving on to bigger and better things.

Or so I'm told.

Daniel Rose

My adventures as Donut Boy started this summer. I wanted to
work in a book or record store, but even the ones that gave me
applications demanded experience. McDonald's and Peoples jobs
seemed too ordinary so, after a few days of sloth, I applied for
the late-night shift at Montgomery Donuts. I was hired for the
afternoons, and trained by a twenty-seven year old woman who
looked sixteen and also worked another job to support her
Nigerian husband. Things have only gotten stranger.

The previous three summers I had attended the Johns
Hopkins Center for Talented Youth held at Dickinson College.
There, I made life-long friends, fell in love with my teachers,
and woke most mornings at five to write. At the end of my last
year, the head of the writing program told me I was the best
student she ever had. I consider my success at Montgomery
Donuts an equal achievement. I was raised to fit in with gifted
children and college professors; I have learned on my own to
deal with the real world.

I work Sunday mornings with the assistant managers, Mildred
Albert and Kathy Gianotas. They are twenty-year veterans of
the donut wars who know half the customers by name, get on
their knees to scrub, and listen to country music on the store's
transistor radio. "Now Daniel," Mildred lectured me one
morning after I'd bagged a chocolate cruller upside down, "you
got to treat yer donuts like you treat yer women—gentle but
fast." Kathy, snaggle-toothed and cackle-laughed, flirts with the
old men, and pats my back every time I pass her on my way
from the eclairs to the honey wheats. I respect them both
because they can pour two medium coffees simultaneously and
work fifty-hour weeks. They respect me because I'm friendly and
don't talk back. They are happy to hear I plan to go to college,
but much happier that I plan to work over Christmas break.

I like working the afternoons better, when I'm alone.
Customers come in one or two at a time, and I write in my
journal to pass the time. There are kids with change enough for

one plain glazed, old people who make sure I pour exactly the right amount of cream, men in dirty work shirts who order coconut fruit logs, sleek women who want a diet coke and grimace when I suggest a donut. With my regular customers, I talk about the weather, hot cars, James Joyce, what's wrong with kids in America today, anything that's on their minds. The day goes by in eight-cent increments, in terms of small, medium, and large.

"Now Daniel," Mildred said the last time our shifts overlapped, "I want the floor mopped good, and the coffee made, and the stock put away. Andy cleaned the cabinets yesterday, so I want you to wash the garbage cans. Inside and out."

"Yes ma'am." I smiled. She stubbed out her Camel unfiltered, put on a bulky coat over her white uniform and orthopedic shoes, patted my upper arm. "And Daniel, I put you in for a raise."

The slip said: Merit Increase. Good with customers. Dependable. Salary to $4.30.

More than enough thanks for Donut Boy.

Essays About the College Application Process

We all love to read about ourselves, so it should come as no surprise that a lot of college admissions officers recommended essays that were about—you guessed it—college admissions. And, also no surprise, a popular way for applicants to discuss the admissions process is with satire. Many essays exaggerate the trials and tribulations of hapless students caught in the most anxious time of their lives—all to great comic effect.

If your point is valid, don't worry about pulling punches. Most admissions officers we talked with would rather be offended than bored. No one seems to get penalized for having fun with the admissions process.

However, we do have a caveat. We understand that essays about the admissions process are becoming more common. Often, they are the lazy way out. That is, the applicant can't think of a good topic, so he writes a clumsy, silly piece about how brutal it is to apply to college. That's a real mistake. As one admissions officer said, "The only thing that really irritates me is when a student puts no thought into the essay." If the essay says too much about the admissions process and not enough about you, you've wasted a valuable opportunity.

The first essay, a poem, is both whimsical and intellectual. "I have to believe the student had a great time writing this," an admissions officer noted. "You'll notice that the essay really doesn't discuss the student at all. It is so clever and amusingly written, however, that from it, one cannot help but draw the conclusion that the student is a witty and easygoing person who chose to poke fun at the college admissions process rather than become anxious about it." But be careful. A poem like this can offer an amusing break for the reader, but it is very gimmicky, and gimmicks can be a substitute for real effort. Unless you, too, are a naturally witty scholar, you probably should discuss yourself more directly.

One admissions officer declared Marjorie Just's piece about writing an essay her all-time favorite. "It is craftily written and uniquely successful in engaging the reader and conveying what the writer is like. I love the fairly easygoing self-consciousness of the essay as it describes not only the anxiety of essay writing for college applications themselves, but also her feelings about herself and her family."

Ingrid Marie Geerken misspelled "Hemingway"—the type of gaffe that can really hurt if your application is assigned to a stickler for detail—but the essay is so witty and creative that the University of North Carolina saved it as one of their favorites.

Michael D. Schill's cartoon is another risky gimmick that works, not because he's an especially talented cartoonist, but because the format shows he's confident enough to "break the mold" and because the content of the cartoon offers real insight into his personality. Basically, Michael wrote a good essay—and made it great by wrapping it in a cartoon.

The last essay is a hilarious takeoff on the whole essay-writing process and the anxiety associated with it—a great essay on which to end the book, we think.

Nicholas Karno

A Shadow in the Light

By Nicholas Karno
(A playful story about a withered Rogue trying to resist
filling the applications that the King of Admissions
wants completed for the Holy Grail of College Entrance)

I've duelled the devil's champion
And kissed the feet of truth;
I've sampled Hamlet's madness when
I robbed the bank of youth.

I've traveled many arid deserts
Crying drops of water.
Too late thou Holy Christian Man!
I ran and stole your daughter.

'Round circumference, in a cycle,
Return thy starting line!
Quench my chaffing indiscretion
And bathe that monster, Time.

Away thy good man Guildenstern,
Leave me, Rosencrantz.
I have no patience for the likes
Of petty happenstance.

What is it now? Can't you see?
I need to be alone!
I swear to you, I'll kill the man
Who breaks into my home!

[Coincidence, I know you're near,

I vaguely see your face.
Your distance strains my eye to view
The color of your race.]

"Oh Sir! Oh Sir! Important news
Of needs so foul and rotten!
Apparently there's no escape,
The bureau's not forgotten.

"The King's commands are prompt and clear,
And not to be confused.
Now fill the application here,
The King won't be refused.

"Come now Sir, your time is up.
What now shall it be?
A risk of giving yourself whole,
Or life in misery?

"Here now are your diff'rent oils,
Brushes and a canvas.
The King wants you to paint your life,
In representing stanzas.

"After that you lick the stamp,
Sign on the dotted line.
Return the printed envelope
To Mercury by nine."

Ha, Ha, Ha! Why that's a laugh!
I'll give you no such thing.
I'll be dammed if you will see
My naked soul of burning.

Try and Try! I will not budge!
You can't unfold my arms!
What's this? Blast it! Stop that noise!
My conscience set alarms.

All right, All right! I give up!
I'm yielding to your King.

But let me warn, my blood runs hot
And he may feel its sting.

I've warned you right, now take a chance.
Look into despair.
Look into my pluvial pit,
You'll find my love down there.

You'll see my love, my hate, my hand
Clenched in a fist.
You'll see a bowl of lucky charms.
An angel I once kissed.

You'll see wars and victories
Fought for manly pride.
You'll see fears, the blackest kind,
And then you'll want to hide.

So take a chance, I dare you now.
Step into my mind.
Then you'll become someone like me,
Trapped in endless rhyme.

Marjorie Just

I paused for a moment, staring at the paper. Hoo, I thought, I think I've read this question a hundred times and I still hyperventilate. What can I tell them that the rest of my application can't? I'm nice. I'm funny. I can be really damn funny when I want to be . . . I care a lot about my friends. And about my family. And I can do a few impressions when I act like a ham. But I can't say this stuff in an essay. It's not original, eyecatching, or witty. I can't be funny by trying really hard. No, funny is out. Don't even try it. It won't work. The college counselor said to be original and not just to summarize a trip you took. That would be a disaster because the admissions people read hundreds of them.

I heard my father coming up the steps. I knew it was Dad because every night around 9:00 he would trudge up the stairs. And before he got ready for bed, he would either ask me to do him a favor or he would go into each room on that floor and see how the room was doing. I knew he was doing the second because he always went to my brother's room first and he was in there now.

"How we doing, Tom?" he said.

"Fine."

"Let's go over the Latin vocabulary together."

"Dad, I'm doing science right now, all-right?"

He closed Tom's door. Here we go, I thought.

He opened the door and leaned into the room. "How we doing?"

"Okay."

"Do you think you'll have some time this weekend to go over math with Tom?"

I thought about the last time I tried to help Tom with math. And the fight we had gotten into because he thought I was being bossy. And the time before that. And the fight we had gotten into then about the same thing. But I like math so I said, "Sure," and hoped Tom would be in a better mood.

134

"Thanks," he said, "he really looks up to you. I know it's hard to tell sometimes because he's trying to be cool. But he cares about what you think so try not to be very critical."

I nodded. I don't know what he's talking about, I thought, I get the feeling he feels exactly the opposite.

"What are you doing?" he asked.

"I'm working on the essay."

"Oh," he said. Not a short "oh" of comprehension, but a long let-me-tell-you-what-I-think "oh."

Here it comes again, I thought.

"You know, you've had some unique experiences these past two summers, going to Finland and working in France."

Again I nodded. It was useless to tell him that it was a bad idea because he had a point to get across (even though it was the same point for the fifth time), and if I didn't let him finish completely, he would call me stubborn and start a fight. Or even worse, he would tell me that it was fine if I didn't want him to talk. He just wouldn't talk to me at all, then. Yes, Dad, say it, I thought, come on: "comparing the two trips would be interesting."

"Maybe you might like to compare the two trips. Talk about the differences between living with a French family and living with a Finnish family."

"Yeah. I'll think about it, Dad, but it has to be something original, not an 'I had a great vacation' thing."

"Yes," he said, "it's important to show that, just like any other seventeen year old, you have fears and insecurities. You're human for goodness sake . . ." He looked up at the ceiling for a moment.

Uh oh, I thought, it's acting time. He's pretending he's me writing the essay. God, he's so melodramatic.

". . . In Finland, though I did not have the comfort of knowing the language, as I did in France, I felt much more secure in Finland, for I did not have any responsibility there. In France, however, I was in charge of a boy and a girl, being an au pair girl, and I had to give them a feeling of security while, at the same time, feeling insecure myself about the society."

I nodded. That's the stupidest, most infantile piece of crap I have ever heard, I thought, it also has about six conjunctions that don't belong, and is about as dull as a flat pancake. You really have no idea how I felt these past two summers, have you?

"Do you know what I mean?" he said. "Obviously, this is just a rough idea, but do you see what I mean?"

"Yeah. I'll try, Dad, but I'm not sure if I'll write about Finland or France."

"Well, I think it would be a good idea. They were both great experiences." He closed the door and went to his room.

I thought, it's amazing the non-conversations I have with him. I just nod and nod and pretend to agree. Everyone spoke English in Finland. I had no real problem with the language. And I worked in Finland every day in Mrs. Sillanpaa's store. I just never minded it.

I got up from my desk and went downstairs to the kitchen where my mom was grading papers.

"Hi, Mom."

"Hi, Honey. How are you doing?" I went over and gave her a hug. The nice thing about hugging my mom is that sometimes she needs it as much as I do.

"I don't know," I said. "I'm trying to write my essay and I don't really know what to write about. I want to write something good and revealing and all that."

"Well, how about the time in elementary school when you asked the teacher to give the girls equal time on the playing field?"

"Mom, I was about nine years old and I don't remember it."

"Oh," she giggled. "How about Finland?"

"I don't know. I don't think it would be very good but Dad thinks it's a great idea. He even started acting it out, you know?"

She smiled. "He does like to do that. But, Honey, you know you should only write what you feel comfortable with. Probably some experience where you learned something, but it doesn't have to be a big revelation."

"Yeah, all-right. I get it. It's just kind of scary to start. But writing about Finland would just come out stupid."

"I don't think so," said my father, standing in the doorway of the kitchen. I quickly turned to face him.

"Dad, I thought you went to bed."

"Why don't you think you can write about Finland," he stated.

I knew he didn't think there was an answer, so he didn't

bother to ask me. He just stated it. I shrugged my shoulder. "I just don't think it would tell enough about me personally. I mean, I had a lot of fun, but my personality didn't change or anything."

"Oh, Marjorie," he whined in his why-do-you-have-to-bug-me-with-this voice, "would you stop scholtzing around and write the goddamn essay on Finland?" When he said this, he did something that always scares me. While he was yelling, he first threw his hands in the air. Then he put his hands on both sides of his face which had turned red. Then he turned to me, bent over so his head was just over mine, and shook his hands, palms up, in front of my face when he said "Goddamn essay."

"Dad?" I said as loudly as he had. I took a step back and looked at my mom.

"Harold, let her write what she thinks is best."

"Marion." He gave her a familiar look that meant he didn't want to see his wife contradicting him.

"No, Hal, she's right. The admissions people don't want to hear a travellogue." My dad's eyes widened and his face turned a brighter shade of red. "She wants to write something more personal than that."

"I did not spend all that money sending her to Finland so she could write about something more personal!!"

"What?!" I was so surprised and angry I wanted to punch him. "What the hell are you talking about? I did not go to Finland so I would have something to write about! I went there and had a great time! It wasn't an educational experience! And my Finnish family was so wonderful and loving that I didn't have any stupid insecurities about the society! But you don't know that because you never asked me how I felt there! You didn't! I can't believe it." I took a big breath and calmed down a little. "Dad. I'm going to write about my personality. I want to show them a little of myself, not my accomplishments."

"I see your trip to Finland as something unique about yourself." I looked at the floor. There was no point arguing if he wasn't going to try to see my side.

I quietly said, "I'm not going to write about Finland and I'm not going to submit it for your approval. I appreciate your wanting to help me but I think I can and should speak for myself." I left the kitchen and went up to my room. I read the essay question and then began to write:

"I paused for a moment, staring at the paper. Hoo, I thought, I think I've read this question a hundred times and I still hyperventilate . . ."

Ingrid Marie Geerken

Once Upon a falling October, screechingly close to when all post secondary applications were due, a girl in red hightops, (preferring to write in the third person), sat down to explain who she was (who *was* she?) on a blank, square piece of paper. She thought (this was done with an alarming frequency) how she yearned to fling herself across that little, but, oh, so very demanding, white essay space, seal herself up snugly in a rectangular envelope—lift the gooey flap before it slammed shut, slide her arm out the back, and stamp it right in the corner. If her mom were home—she'd ask her politely to address the envelope and send it off to the **Undergraduate Admissions, Monogram Building 153-A, Country Club Road, Chapel Hill, N.C. 27514.**

On second thought (something she also had with an alarming frequency) she thought that writers are so temperamental that she would probably crumple up and throw herself away.

"Where are they when I need them!?" she cried in delirious desperation, groping for the heroes living on her shelves, lounging luxuriously inside her books, rooming comfortably with their settings, characters, plots, themes, styles, tones, ironies and symbolisms.

"Certainly their words chisled a glimpse of human nature into a monument of truth. Surely, they could write a classic—but, the question is—could they write a college essay?"

If you wish, use the following space to provide information about yourself which you think may help us in making our decision. Please add extra sheets if necessary.

What would Hemmingway write? I mused.

My name is Ernest. I am a man. I am a writer. I would like to attend the University of North Carolina. At Chapel Hill.

Presenting Faulkner.

The name given to me at the moment of glorious birth when the fruits of the conception that were created through the guiding hands of the most Holy Being through the act of ultimate love between those who gave me life is the striking and most beautiful appellate of William Faulkner.

e.e. cummings in the Spotlight:

mY (N)a(ME) !!! E.?e. (is)
sgnimmuC.
i a　　　　m. a
(poet.)(.)
i.

Though he claimed that brevity was the soul of wit, Shakespeare always had a way with words:

The wheel of fortune hath spun—that arrant whore bestowed upon me the most wretched of inquiries. Thy wit shall not go slipshod. Hear me committee—set less than thou trowest. I owest thou naught my name. Go to, have thy wisdom; it is William Shakespeare.

J.D. Salinger is a favorite of mine:

Damn it! Why the hell are you asking my name? Phonies are always asking crap like that. I don't know why, but they get a goddamn kick out of asking people who they are and what their names are and if they have a permanent mailing address. Those phony bastards really kill me. They want to know what you're goddamn address is so that they can send you a goddamn letter saying that you're not good enough for them. Things like that really depress me.

David Thoreau meditates:

Why I was named David Thoreau. With respectful civil disobedience, I must defer this question until I have gone into the woods and contemplated the matter more thoroughly. (thoreau-ly.) UNC. "There I might live, I said . . ."

Freud insists:

My identification is goal-oriented with a small tendency toward narcissism. My Id, Ego, and Superego are all fully developed and the most predominant defense mechanism of my ego is projection. (For example, If I am not accepted into the University of North Carolina At Chapel Hill, I will utilize my ability to blame it on

140

outside or extenuating circumstances, and I will say, They don't know a good essay when they see one.*) Because of my pleasure derived from relieving myself during the Anal stage of development, I am basically an outgoing person. I chew on my pen caps because some of my libido was stunted in the oral stage of development.*

Arthur Miller dramatizes:
BEN: *Why, boys, when I was seventeen I walked into the University of North Carolina at Chapel Hill and when I was twenty-one I walked out.* He laughs. *And by God I was wise!*
WILLY: *"You see what I been talking about? The greatest things can happen!"*

I say, (says she, switching from third to first person) that my name is Ingrid. I think too much, I laugh too loud, I live intensely. Heaven for me would be to be locked up in a small room with stacks and piles and reams of blank paper; Hell for me would be to be locked up in a small room with stacks and piles and reams of blank sheets of white paper, without a pencil, pen, typewriter, piece of chalk, crayon, carbon, paint, or any other type of writing utensil. It's equivalent to locking Michaelangelo up in a room with thousands of pure marble blocks and refusing to give him a chisel. (The situations are equivalent—not the artists.)

When I go to college, (Will UNC have anything to do with me?), I have decided that I will bring forth from my room these things: 1)The complete works of J.D. Salinger, 2)*A Separate Peace* by John Knowles, 3)*A Winters Tale* by Mark Helprin, 4)Poetry by Carl Sandburg and T.S. Eliot, 5)My poster of the statue of David by Michelangelo, 6)Mickey Mouse and my Teddy Bear, 6)My watercolors, 7)My Talking Head Albums, 8)My newspapers, my yearbook (My unsigned yearbooks. I always hated signing them). 9)My English teacher's address. 10)Myself.

My name is Ingrid and more than anything else in the world right now, I want to become a part of the University of North Carolina at Chapel Hill.

141

Michael D. Schill

Name Withheld

The Office of Admissions S.W.A.T. Team was travelling through St. Louis on Wednesday at four P.M. cracking down on prospective students, randomly busting in on unsuspecting kids. The team had already visited several candidates, all of whom were in the middle of helping elderly people with their groceries, but there was one more to go . . .

I was unfortunate enough to have been in the game room at Tropicana Lanes when it happened. I was playing Cyclone, a pinball game which had an amusement park theme, and a barker who occasionally yelled at me: "You pays your money, you takes your chances." or more rarely, "We have a winnaaar!" Well, there I was, quite intent upon getting the replay at 1.3 million, when I was flanked by a couple of people in Brooks Brothers suits who flashed badges at me. One said commandingly, "Swarthmore S.W.A.T.: Admissions Officer. Just calmly keep on playing and be yourself." I knew then that I was in for some questioning. Their first question hurt, "So is this what you do with your life?" I tried to explain that they had caught me at a bad time, that this was the first time I had been to Tropicana in months—maybe years, but they cut me off and bruised me with another. "Can you tell us about people who have influenced you?" I slapped the metal ball up onto the ferris-wheel. A happy tune played. My brain rushed to find an answer: Washington, Lincoln, Reagan! Aaahhaa . . . Dukakis! But instead I said, "Well, there's this friend of mine, Mark, who is inspired in just about everything he does. He sings and plays saxophone for the band I'm in, and the other day we were making some tapes, but things started dragging a bit. As a result, none of us could get the song to click. So, after about the fourth take, Mark started practically screaming the vocals and jumping all around. Suddenly I was into it. We were all into it, and the song came together. This is the embodiment of his personality: that he becomes involved in something and his involvement inspires others. Recently . . ." "Velcome to my spook house!!" blared the game. I looked up at the face of the man next to me. He looked deathly, like Dracula, and I quickly turned my head back to the game and continued. "Recently I was talking with Mark about whether or not I should join the ice-hockey team. He just lit up and I thought he was going to get up and shake me or something. 'Are you kidding? This may be your last opportunity to be on a team like that. Put on your skates and get out there!' It's funny that my parents later told me the same thing. You see, Mark has no known father, and he's the last person you might expect to be giving fatherly advice, yet it comes out of him as though he's found his father inside." The game 'bing'-ed. Their last question was the hardest, for there I was, playing Cyclone in the game room of Tropicana Lanes, and they asked me, "What are your goals or hopes for the future?" The question overwhelmed me. Which future were they talking about? At one level I wanted to get that replay score, and have another game, but still farther ahead I wanted to get into college, and beyond that were so many things: The environment, peace, my children, the economy, poetry, science, love, music, memories . . . I wanted to be involved in it all; to do everything with the adrenaline that rushed through me at that moment, that adrenaline which shook the pinball game. "Hey! you with the face!" cried the barker. I wondered where I was headed. "Give me the world and I'll feed the starving, and I'll work for peace, and I'll play Beethoven in the slums until there are no slums, and I'll pay off the deficit with money from my own wallet, until I'm the richest poor-man on." TILT

144

Before You Finalize and Mail It

1. Double-check for spelling, grammar, and punctuation mistakes.

2. Check for wordiness. Most essays could make their point more effectively if they were about half as long.

3. Make sure the essay looks neat.

4. Make sure you are satisfied with the essay. Does it reflect your personality and how you want to present yourself? Can you say, "This sounds like me"?

5. Photocopy the essay and the rest of the application, sign it, and mail it. Good luck!

About the Editors

Boykin Curry and Brian Kasbar grew up together in New Jersey and graduated from Yale University in 1988. Boykin now lives in Boston, and Brian lives in Los Angeles.